2/99

Discarded by
Santa Maria Library

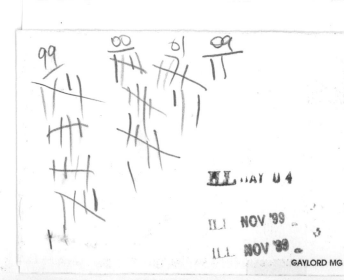

ILL MAY 04

ILI NOV '99

ILL NOV '99

GAYLORD MG

The
SCRAP CRAFT
PROJECT BOOK

The
SCRAP CRAFT
PROJECT BOOK

Nicki Wheeler

David & Charles

For Timmy always

To Goldie and Fluff
with my love

A DAVID & CHARLES BOOK

First published in the UK in 1998

A catalogue record for this book is available from
the British Library.

ISBN 0 7153 0725 8

Photography by Di Lewis
Book design by Maggie Aldred
Illustrations by Penny Brown
and printed in Great Britain by Butler & Tanner
for David & Charles
Brunel House   Newton Abbot   Devon

Contents

Introduction

Fabric scraps, household textiles and basic materials combined with some simple sewing techniques like embroidery, patchwork, appliqué and quilting are used to make all the projects in this book – there are even some projects that involve no sewing at all!

Each project takes a colour or motif as a theme and is illustrated with a beautiful colour photograph. You'll find that each project lists the materials and haberdashery needed, together with full step-by-step instructions. Templates and patterns are at the back of the book, while information on choosing fabrics and using templates and instructions for the techniques and embroidery stitches can be found at the front of the book.

The idea of using fabric scraps is to save you money and put what you already have to good use. All projects use fabric scraps, old clothes and household textiles such as sheets, blankets and curtains; and basic fabrics like calico, hessian (jute), gingham and felt. You don't need large amounts of fabrics for the patchwork and appliqué, so scraps and small fabric pieces are ideal.

If you can't find fabrics in the colours you want, try dying them – it's amazing how a pattern or design can be completely transformed in this way. Indeed, many of the projects use old woollen blankets which look absolutely stunning when dyed and embroidered.

Templates are provided for each project so you can copy the designs given here exactly, but feel free to adapt the designs to fit in with the materials you have at home. If you haven't got quite enough fabric, you can still make many of the projects, using a photocopier to reduce the size of the template patterns until they fit. Likewise, you can enlarge the designs if you wish, or change their colour schemes.

It's always satisfying to make something, but think what fun it is to see scraps of favourite fabrics transformed into toys, accessories or special gifts. I hope this book will supply you with endless inspiration to let your imagination run riot.

Happy stitching,
Nicki Wheeler

Basic Techniques

EQUIPMENT & MATERIALS

You don't need many tools or materials to make the projects in this book, and often you can improvise, using whatever you have already. However, you will find some of the following tools and instructions useful.

Make sure the tools you do have are in good working order – scissors should be sharp and needles clean and free from signs of rust. To save money, look at where you can buy fabrics cheaply or see if you have any old clothes or furnishings you could recycle   you may get much more interesting and exciting results by reusing some older fabrics.

♥

Needles

You'll need a good selection of needles for general hand sewing and embroidery. For tough fabrics, try using leather needles – they'll make it much easier to get through several layers.

Pins

Use long, rust-free pins, such as quilting or glass-headed pins. Glass-headed pins have the advantage of being easy to find and remove.

Thimble

This is useful to protect your fingers and to help push the needle through tough fabrics.

Scissors

Use sharp dressmaker's scissors for cutting out large pieces of fabric and sharp, pointed embroidery scissors for cutting around delicate shapes and trimming off threads. Pinking shears will enable you to create decorative edges in minutes and also help prevent edges fraying. Don't use your fabric scissors for cutting out paper templates because you'll blunt them. Use a separate pair of scissors for this purpose.

Embroidery Frames & Hoops

These can make sewing easier because they keep fabric taught, enabling you to maintain an even tension and ensure stitches lie flat. They come in a range of types and sizes – you'll probably find that the larger ones are the most useful.

Fabrics

You can buy your fabrics new or recycle old garments and soft furnishings. If you don't have any in the colour you want, dye scrap fabric or use fabric paints to add interest (see page 12). Wash and steam press your chosen fabrics to pre-shrink them and to remove any excess dye before you cut them out.

Padding & Stuffing

Some of the items in this book are padded to give them extra body or stuffed to give them shape. For padding use polyester wadding (batting) or old pre-washed blanket. For stuffing, tear up wadding into small pieces and use this, or buy a toy stuffing for the purpose.

Threads

The exact threads used in the projects are rarely specified to encourage you to use up whatever you have already. For hand stitching use stranded embroidery cotton (floss) or tapestry wool (yarn), and for machine stitching use ordinary sewing thread. The Christmas collection in this book includes embroidery in metallic threads, but you don't have to buy these specially – just substitute an ordinary embroidery cotton (floss) in festive red, yellow or green. For projects like patchwork, use complementary threads for machine stitching and a contrasting thread for decorative machine or hand stitching.

Buttons

These are ideal for suggesting the eyes of some of the characters in this book, for representing the sun, melon pips or grapes, and as pure decoration. Use buttons from old clothing or from items bought in charity shops or jumble sales.

Trimmings

Even the smallest oddments of ribbon, lace and braid are useful for the projects here. If you don't have any already, look out for odd bits of bric-a-brac in haberdashery departments, charity shops and jumble sales. If the trimmings aren't new, hand wash and gently press them before use.

PATTERNS & TEMPLATES

All the motifs and patterns used in this book are clearly labelled and can be found on pages 112-126. For some projects you can trace them directly, but for others you will need to enlarge them to size, either using a photocopier or by scaling them up on graph paper as explained below. Details on sizing are provided alongside each template or pattern.

♥

Enlarging or Reducing to Size

The templates are designed to be enlarged or reduced with a photocopier. A degree of enlargement or reduction is suggested as a guide (+200%, or -70%, for example) but you can copy the template to whatever size you want. You can do this yourself or a print shop will do it for you. Alternatively, use graph paper to scale the templates to size by hand as explained here.

1 Trace the design onto paper, draw a box

around it, mark regular points at 1 to 2.5cm ($\frac{1}{2}$ to 1in) intervals along the edges, then join the points to make a grid. Number the boxes along one vertical and one horizontal edge.

2 Draw a larger or smaller box on another piece of paper to the size you want the finished design, draw up a grid in it with the same number of squares as the previous grid, and number them to match.

3 Copy the contents and shapes of each box accurately onto the empty grid, using the numbers along the edges as a guide (fig. 1).

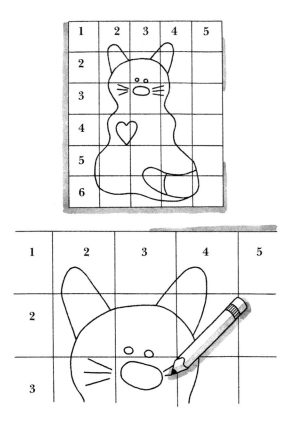

fig. 1 Using a grid

Using Templates

To make a template, trace or photocopy your design, stick the copy onto card or stiff paper, label each shape clearly and cut out.

Some designs are made from several shapes which should be cut from different fabrics. When cutting and attaching these shapes it's easiest to lay the smaller pieces over the larger ones rather than trying to cut shapes accurately and fit them together like a jigsaw puzzle. For example, lay the grass over the Easter bunny shape rather than trying to cut the grass and bunny to fit together. To make the layers, trace each shape separately, label it clearly and cut out (fig. 2). Alternatively, make several photocopies and cut out the appropriate shapes.

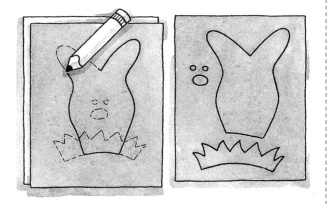

fig. 2 Using templates

Patterns

Some projects use patterns which can be found at the back of the book. To use the patterns, trace off each pattern piece from the book, or enlarge or reduce the pieces as appropriate. Some pattern pieces have been overlapped to fit on the page. Coloured lines have been used where each piece overlaps, so trace over these.

Design Layouts

Some projects use a mixture of templates, embroidery and fabric paints to achieve the finished effect. Templates for these designs are at the back of the book, and design layouts are illustrated alongside the project instructions. Use the illustration as a guide for placing the template and for where to embroider or use fabric marker pens.

To draw your own full-size design layout, draw the template to size, trace this onto a piece of paper, then draw the rest of the design around it, using the illustration as a guide.

Transferring Designs

There are lots of ways to transfer designs onto fabric. Two very simple methods are shown below. Use the method which feels most comfortable for you and is most suitable for the design and fabrics being used. Always work on the right side of the fabric.

Tracing a design against a window

This is a quick way of transferring simple designs to pale-coloured, light or medium-weight fabrics. With right sides facing up, tape the paper design to a sunny window, then tape the fabric over this. Use a pencil or dressmaker's chalk pencil to trace the design onto the fabric. If you can't see the design through the fabric properly, remove it and use a black marker pen to draw round the design on the paper. Now try tracing it again. To reverse the design, stick the paper design to the window with the right side against the glass. If necessary, trace over the design lines on the back of the paper before transferring it to the fabric.

Using dressmaker's carbon

This is ideal for tracing complex designs, and works best on smooth fabrics because lines can become fuzzy on rougher fabrics. Dressmaker's carbon is available from haberdashery shops in a variety of colours and can be removed by washing the fabric in cold water. Choose a colour close to the fabric colour, but with enough contrast to show up. Never use ordinary office carbon which is indelible.

1 With right sides up, tape the fabric to a hard, flat surface, then tape the design over the fabric. Carefully slip the carbon between the two layers, with the coloured side facing down.

2 Use a ball-point pen or knitting needle to trace around all the lines of the design. Now and then, carefully lift one corner of the design to see if you are using enough pressure to ensure that the design comes through to the fabric.

DECORATIVE STITCHES

All the stitches used in the projects are quite straightforward. However, if you haven't worked some of the stitches before or if you need a quick reminder, you'll find the instructions here invaluable. If you wish, you can use your favourite embroidery stitches rather than those recommended in the project instructions. If you'd rather avoid hand stitching altogether, either use machine stitching or create fake stitching by using a fabric marker pen to imitate the look of the stitches (see page 12).

♥

Backstitch

This stitch is useful for lettering or for outlining shapes and it is strong enough to use for seams instead of machine stitching. Referring to fig. 3, bring the needle through the fabric at 1. In one movement, insert the needle to the right at 2 and then bring it out to the left of 1 at 3, so that 3 is the same distance from 1 as 2. Repeat to work a line of stitches.

fig. 3 Working backstitch

Blanket stitch

Use this decorative stitch for finishing edges and outlining appliqué motifs. The effect should be bold, so work the stitch in tapestry yarn or with several strands of embroidery cotton (floss) and make the stitches fairly large and widely spaced. Bring the needle through the fabric at 1 or at the fabric edge (see fig. 4). In one movement, insert the needle at 2 and then bring it back out at 3.

Wrap the thread loop under the needle and then gently pull the needle through. Repeat to work a line of parallel, regular stitches.

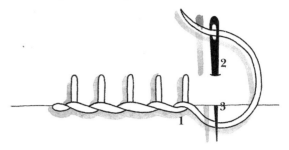

fig. 4 Working blanket stitch

Cross stitch

This simple stitch has a host of uses in this book, from creating decorative borders to adding flower centres and animal features. Working in an imaginary square, bring the needle out at the bottom right and insert it at the top left. Now bring the needle out at the bottom left and insert it at the top right to complete the stitch (see fig. 5). To create a row or border of cross stitches, work a row of diagonal stitches one way, then work back in the opposite direction to complete the crosses.

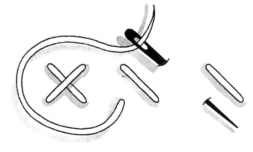

fig. 5 Working cross stitch

Lazy-daisy stitch

This pretty stitch is useful for petals, grass and leaves. Referring to fig. 6, above right, bring the needle up at 1, go back through close to where the thread emerged, without pulling the thread right through. Now bring the needle point through at 2. Loop the thread under the needle point and bring the needle through, pulling the

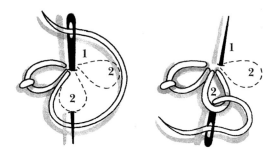

fig.6 Working lazy-daisy stitch

thread so the loop is the required size. In one movement, insert the needle close by to catch the loop in place, then bring it out close to 1, ready to start the next stitch.

Running stitch

Use this stitch for borders, quilting or outlining shapes. Working from right to left, 'run' the needle in and out of the fabric, making evenly spaced stitches of the same size (see fig. 7).

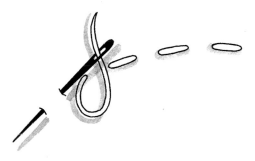

fig. 7 Working running stitch

Straight stitch

Worked in any length or direction, these versatile stitches are useful for capturing grass, flowers and stars. Bring the needle through to the right side of the fabric at the starting posi-

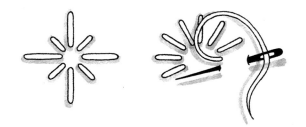

fig. 8 Working straight stitch

tion and take it back through to the wrong side at the finish (see fig. 8). To suggest a daisy flower or the sun's rays, work equally spaced stitches in a circle; to create a star, work four long straight stitches radiating from a single point with four shorter diagonal stitches between them.

Oversewing

This isn't technically a decorative stitch, but it is used in this book and therefore deserves a mention. Use it for hemming or to attach appliquéd motifs. Working from right to left with the needle horizontal, pick up a few threads in the main fabric and then a few threads from the hem or appliqué motif. Repeat to work tiny stitches quite close together (see fig. 9).

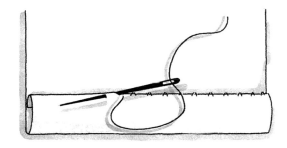

fig.9 Working oversewing

DYES, MARKER PENS & PAINTS

Fabric dyes, marker pens and paints enable you to transform fabrics in double-quick time. Use dyes to change the fabric completely, or choose paints or pens to add a few embellishments, applying the paint with a brush, stamp or stencil according to preference. Follow the manufacturer's instructions and test the paints and pens on a scrap of the fabric before starting your design.

♥

Testing Fabrics

Most dyes and paints work best with fabrics made from natural fibres – some synthetics resist the colour – so try to use fabrics made from cotton, linen, wool, silk or viscose. If you don't know what the fabric is made of, test the dye, fabric paint or marker pen on a small scrap of fabric first.

Fabric Dyes

These come in two basic types – one for hand dyeing and one for use in a washing machine. Use hand dyes for small amounts or very delicate fabrics and machine dyes for large items, such as blankets or sheets. Wool absorbs a lot of dye, so either dye once for a soft shade or twice for a stronger colour.

Fabric Marker Pens

These provide a quick-and-easy way to add writing and detail to a design. They look like felt-tip pens and come in a number of basic colours from good craft suppliers. All you do is mark your design on the fabric and then leave to dry. Turn the fabric over and iron it to fix the colour.

You can use marker pens to imitate embroidery stitches by applying them in broken lines – see the patchwork cot cover on page 56. If you wish, stitch over the marked lines to emphasize the design. Alternatively, use pen on some areas of the project and embroider others – that way you can combine the speed and freedom of pens with the hand-crafted look of embroidery.

Marker pens are also useful for adding small details, such as the eyes, mouth and whiskers of the juggling cats (page 28) and for messages in the greetings cards and hangings. For the starlight picture (page 58), the writing was done with a gold marker pen and then stitched over with gold thread. Gold and silver marker pens can't be fixed, so only use them for projects that don't require washing.

Fabric Paints

There are two groups of fabric paints, one designed for painting on silk and the other for cotton or cotton-mix fabrics – you'll need the latter. These generally come in small jars and look and behave just like poster paints – you can even mix colours together and dilute them with water. Apply them with an artist's brush or use a stamp or stencil.

You can buy ready-made stamps and stencils for use with fabrics and fabric paints, but for the chess board on page 111 you will need to make a potato block stamp as explained below. Alternatively, you can make a stencil.

Making a potato block

Find a potato larger than the motif you wish to use as a stamp and cut it in half. Lay the template on the cut surface of the potato and use a knife to cut round the edges. Next cut away the excess potato from the edges to leave a raised block shape (fig. 10). Pour a little fabric paint into a saucer. Dip the block into the fabric paint then stamp the design on the fabric. Leave the paint to dry, then press from the wrong side to fix it. Test the stamp on scrap paper first.

fig. 10 Making a potato block

Making a stencil

Copy the template onto paper, then cut out the shape. Lay the shape on a piece of stiff card and draw round it with a pencil. Use a knife or scissors to cut round the edges of the shape, leaving a cut-out stencil on the card. Lay the stencil over the fabric, then use a sponge or brush to dab fabric paint over the stencil and fabric. Remove the stencil and allow the paint to dry, then press from the wrong side to fix it.

APPLIQUÉ

Appliqué is a method of creating a design by stitching fabric shapes to a base fabric. Decorative hand or machine stitches secure the fabric shapes, and extra detail can be added by using embroidery, fabric marker pens and buttons. There are lots of ways to work appliqué, but the simplest method, using fusible bonding material, is shown below.

♥

Fabrics for Appliqué

Appliqué is a good way of using up fabric scraps, but for practical items avoid delicate fabrics such as silks or stretchy fabrics like lightweight jersey which can be difficult to sew. Use a heavier base fabric with lighter weight scraps for the shapes. You can use virtually any fabrics – even old clothes – but lightweight, closely woven cotton fabrics are easy to use because they tend not to fray much. Washable felt doesn't fray at all.

Fusible Bonding

Fusible bonding makes appliqué simple. It sticks (fuses) fabrics together by melting when heat is applied, and it prevents fraying, making fabric pieces easier to work with. Iron fusible bonding onto fabric, cut out the shapes and then iron them onto the base fabric. For security, and to enhance the design, add decorative hand or machine stitches, topstitching close to the edge of the shape. Fusible bonding material is available from good haberdashery shops (stores).

How to use fusible bonding

Apply the design to the fusible bonding and fabric using one of the two methods described here. When tracing templates, place them with right side down. This reverses the design, so when the shapes are cut out they are the right way round. Symmetrical shapes, such as hearts, circles or squares, don't have to be reversed.

Method one: 1 Lay out the fabric, right side down, and place a matching piece of fusible bonding on top, rough adhesive side down. Press with a hot, dry iron to fuse both layers together. Place your template right side down on the paper side of the bonded fabric, trace each shape, label it and cut it out.

fig. 11 Using fusible bonding

Method two: 1 Place your template right side down, then lay fusible bonding on top, rough adhesive side downwards. Trace the shapes, label and cut them out roughly (fig. 11). Lay the cut-out shapes, rough adhesive side down, over the wrong side of some fabric then iron gently with a hot dry iron to fuse both layers together (fig. 12). Allow the bonded fabric to cool, then cut out the shapes exactly.

2 Remove the paper backing, lay the fabric shapes on top of the base fabric, adhesive side

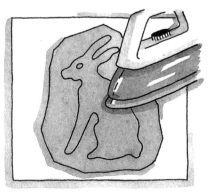

fig. 12 Fusing bonding fabric

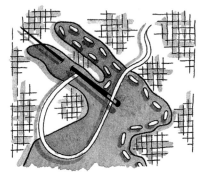

fig. 13 Finishing the shapes

facing downwards, cover with a damp cloth, and iron with a hot dry iron to fuse in place. To finish, work decorative hand or machine stitches round each appliquéd shape (fig. 13).

QUILTING

Quilting is a technique of creating a padded and stitched design. Rows of hand or machine stitches are worked through two layers of fabric, with a padded layer sandwiched in between. This is a useful technique to learn – it's both decorative and practical. The Autumn rabbit cushion (page 98) shows how a design can be created just by outlining the shapes with running stitches in stranded cotton (floss). The nautical bath mat (page 69) uses quilting as a practical way of keeping the layers together – this makes the bath mat more sturdy. Rows of machine stitches strengthen the edges of the mat and outline the appliquéd shapes to give them greater emphasis.

♥

Backing Fabric

Backing fabric forms the bottom piece of the quilting sandwich and secures the central layer of padding. If you're quilting on a cushion where the backing won't be seen, use a lightweight fabric like muslin or cotton, but if you're making something like a bath mat where the back of the design may show, use the same fabric as for the front. This will also make it more durable.

Padding

Polyester wadding (batting) is favoured for quilting because it's lightweight, washable and comes in various weights and widths. There's even an iron-on wadding (batting) available. Old woollen blankets are a practical alternative, but they're slightly heavier in weight. Whichever padding you use, make sure it's washable. If you're using old blankets or thick woollen cloth, hand wash it first to pre-shrink it.

Threads

Any threads can be used for quilting, depending on the effect you're trying to achieve. For hand stitching use sewing or stranded embroidery cotton (floss) in a matching or contrasting colour. For machine quilting use ordinary sewing thread or strong quilting thread, and for decorative work use machine embroidery thread.

How to quilt

1 Cut a piece of fabric slightly larger than the finished size, then cut a piece of both padding and backing fabric to the same size. Transfer the design to the right side of the top piece of fabric (see page 9 and fig. 14).

2 Sandwich the padding between the two fabrics with the design facing up. Pin and tack (baste) all three layers together, starting at the centre and working out towards the edges.

3 For the quilting, stitch along the lines of the design, either by machine or by hand, using

fig. 14 Transferring the design

small running stitches or backstitch. When the quilting is complete, remove the tacking (basting) threads and any visible markings, then press. Transfer markings can usually be rubbed away, but for stubborn marks, gently hand wash in cold water.

PATCHWORK

Patchwork is a method of joining small pieces of fabric together to make a larger piece. It's an ideal way of using up odd fabric scraps, old children's clothes or treasured fabric scraps to make special gifts with sentimental value. Fabric pieces in simple shapes like squares or rectangles fit together easily – follow the instructions below, and don't worry if the shapes don't look perfectly neat, it's all part of the charm of the technique.

♥

Choosing Fabrics

Select fabrics in complementary colours and designs. They may all share a colour or motif which helps them blend well. Ideally, use fabrics of a similar weight and fibre content so the patchwork can be easily cleaned. Lightweight fabrics like cotton and wool are ideal.

How to make a patchwork

1 Decide on the size and shape of the patchwork blocks. Make a template by drawing round each shape on stiff paper or card, then add a 1cm (1/2in) seam allowance all round. Cut out and use it as a pattern to cut out the fabric.

2 Lay the fabric pieces right side down on a flat surface, then use a pencil or dressmaker's chalk to draw round the templates and mark out their shapes. Cut out all the pieces you need in a selection of fabrics.

3 Before joining the shapes, arrange them on a flat surface in the correct order to check you have created the right effect with the fabrics, and also that you have cut enough pieces.

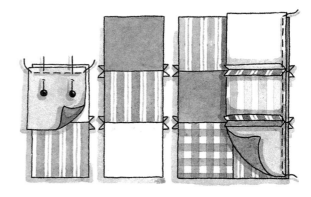

fig. 15 Joining patches

4 To join the pieces, pin two patches together with right sides facing, then tack (baste) and stitch along one edge, taking a 1cm (1/2in) seam allowance. Continue joining more fabric patches in the same way until you have a strip as long as you need (fig. 15). Press seams open.

fig. 16 Adding the border sections

5 Make more strips of patches, then join the strips in the same way. Continue until all the strips are joined, then press the seams open. When you're making an item which has a central patchwork or appliquéd panel and a patchwork border round the edge, work the central panel first, then add the border sections (fig. 16).

Using patchwork fabric

If you are making an item from patchwork fabric, such as the patchwork heart cushion (see page 36) start by making a large piece of patchwork fabric. Press the seams open, then use the patchwork like a normal piece of fabric, pinning your pattern on the fabric and cutting round it.

FINISHING OFF

The way you finish an item can often be the making of it. Well-made openings and attractive borders or bindings can help to give an item a professional look.

♥

Cushions & Covers

Although you can easily make cushion covers which aren't removable, you'll find it's worth making removable versions because they are simpler to clean and iron.

Making a removable cover

Cut the front the required size of your cushion or cover, adding 1.5cm (⅝in) seam allowances all round. For the back, cut two pieces, each the same width but only two-thirds the length of the front shape, and hem one long edge of each piece. Lay the back pieces over the front piece with right sides facing and hems overlapping at the centre. Stitch all round, taking a 1.5cm (⅝in) seam allowance. Trim the seam allowances at the corners and turn right sides out. The back pieces overlap to form the opening (fig. 17).

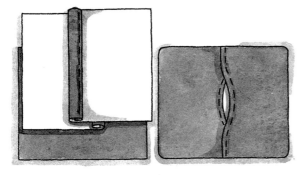

fig. 17 Attaching the back pieces

Borders

Fabric borders are made from overlapping fabric strips stitched to the centre panel of fabric to form a decorative frame. Projects with borders are finished off with backing fabric – the project instructions tell you how to do this.

Attaching a border

1 On a piece of paper, draw the size and shape of the finished item. Decide how wide you want the border, then mark its position on your paper pattern – draw the side border sections first, then mark the top and bottom borders. (fig.18).

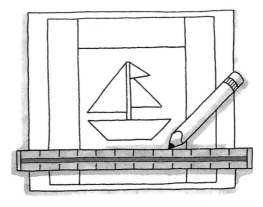

fig 18 Marking the border

2 Cut fabric strips the size of the border sections, adding 1.5cm (⅝in) seam allowances all round. Lay the centre panel face up and pin the top and bottom border strips on top, with right sides down. Stitch along the seams, then fold the strips back to hide the stitching so all pieces are now right sides up. Now join the side strips in the same way as the top and bottom strips, but with the edges overlapping the top and bottom border strips (fig. 19). When all four strips are stitched in place, follow the project instructions to add the backing fabric.

fig. 19 Joining the border

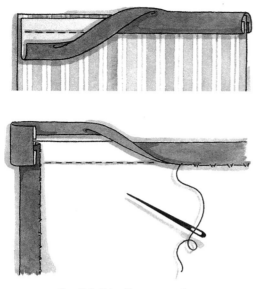

fig 20 Binding an edge

Bias Binding

Attaching bias binding is a decorative and practical way of finishing raw edges and keeping them neat. Straight edges can be bound with strips of fabric, ribbon or braid cut on the straight grain, but for curved edges use bias binding, which you can purchase ready-made or make yourself, following the instructions below.

Making and attaching binding

1 Measure the length of the edges to be bound to work out how much binding you will need. Add a little extra to allow for turnings. Work out how wide you want the binding to be, double this measurement, then add 3cm (1¼in) for turnings – for a 2.5cm (1in) wide binding you will need to cut 8cm (3¼in) wide strips. For bias strips see Cutting bias strips, right.

2 To form the binding, press 1.5cm (⅝in) turnings to the wrong side along each long edge, then bring the folds together, enclosing the raw edges and press. The binding is now ready for you to use.

3 Make a row of tacking (basting) stitches along the edge to be bound – if your finished binding is 2.5cm (1in) wide, the tacking (basting) stitches should be 2.5cm (1in) from the edge. Open the

folded edges of the binding, lay it along the edge to be bound with right sides facing and the fold line along the tacked (basted) line. Pin, tack (baste) and stitch along the fold line. Turn the binding to the wrong side and fold in the raw edge so it covers the line of machine stitches (fig. 20). Slipstitch it in place.

4 When binding all four edges of a square or rectangle, you'll find it easiest to bind two opposite sides first, trimming away any excess fabric at the ends. Stitch the binding to the remaining sides of the fabric, extending the binding by 1cm (½in) at each end. Fold in the excess fabric at each bound end, then slipstitch the binding in place as before.

Cutting bias strips

To cut bias strips, take a fairly large piece of fabric and fold in a corner at a 45 degree angle. Cut along the diagonal fold to find the fabric bias. Now use a chalk pencil and ruler to draw diagonal lines, parallel with your first cut, to the required width of your binding (fig. 21). Cut along the lines to make bias strips.

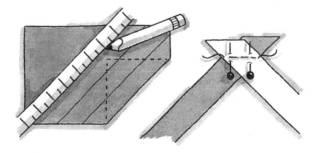

fig. 21 Cutting bias binding

To join the bias strips, pin them at right angles, right sides together, so the short ends match (fig 21). Stitch them together across the ends, taking a small seam allowance – 6-10mm (¼-⅜in) – then press the seam open and trim away the excess fabric at the seam. Continue joining the strips until you have the length you need – it is usually best to make more than enough to allow for turnings.

Sunflower kitchen

*L*ovely bright yellow sunflowers bring a touch of sunshine to any kitchen. This colourful project combines patchwork and simple appliquéd sunflowers to create a cheerful collection of practical kitchen accessories. All you need is a little imagination to transform basic fabrics like hessian (jute), calico, gingham and felt – or even colourful fabric scraps and old household textiles – into beautiful designs. You'll be amazed how easy it can be. Old woollen blankets make an ideal lining for a tea cosy or patchwork oven gloves, or provide a heat-absorbent base for place mats; and an old shirt and odd buttons form the petals and seeds on the sunflower banner which is hung from a stick found on a woodland walk. So let your imagination run away with you and bring a breath of summer sunshine to your kitchen.

Tea-cosy

WHAT YOU NEED:

Paper and pencil
Ruler • Scissors
Hessian (jute)
Pre-washed old woollen
blanket - or wadding
(batting) and lining
Photocopy of sunflower and
leaf templates (see
page 115)
Fusible bonding
Fabric scraps • Iron
Sewing thread and pins
Decorative bias binding

1 Make a paper pattern for the tea-cosy by drawing round an existing tea-cosy. Alternatively, draw a 36 x 26cm (14 x 10in) rectangle; mark a point on each short edge of the rectangle 10cm (4in) down from the top long edge, then draw a curved line to join each point to the top long edge.

2 Cut two shapes from hessian (jute) for the tea-cosy front and back, and two from blanket for the linings. If you prefer not to use blanket, cut two shapes each from wadding (batting) and lining fabric.

3 Using the photocopied sunflower and leaf templates as patterns, trace three flower shapes, three flower centres and six leaves onto fusible bonding. Iron the bonding onto the wrong side of contrasting fabric scraps and cut out the shapes. Peel away the backing and arrange the fabric shapes on the hessian (jute) tea-cosy front. Iron them in place, then secure the shapes with machine stitching.

4 To make the tea-cosy, lay the front and back pieces, right sides up, over a lining piece. If you're using wadding (batting), sandwich it between the two layers. Pin and tack (baste) the layers all around the edges. Bind the long straight edge of each piece with decorative bias binding (see page 17). With right sides up, pin the front and back pieces together, tack (baste) and stitch around the curved edge. Finish this edge with decorative bias binding.

Teapot stand

WHAT YOU NEED:

Scissors
Tape measure or ruler
Calico
Wadding (batting)
Fabric marker pen
Fusible bonding • Iron
Fabric and felt scraps
Sewing thread
Essential oil

1 Cut two 24cm (9½in) squares of calico and one of wadding (batting). On one calico square use a fabric marker pen to draw a broken line 5cm (2in) in from each edge. Copy the sunflower and leaf templates from page 115, and use fusible bonding and scrap fabric to appliqué a sunflower to the centre of the square and a leaf to each corner square. Use a fabric marker pen to write 'Sunflower' in each remaining rectangle.

2 Lay the completed design, right side up, over the square of wadding (batting), then lay the remaining calico square on top of the completed design. Pin and machine stitch around the edges, leaving a gap for turning. Trim the seam allowances at the corners. Turn the square right sides out, then machine stitch close to the edge and along the drawn lines. Finish by sprinkling a few drops of essential oils on the flower centre – the scent will be released as it is warmed by the teapot.

Place mats

WHAT YOU NEED:

Paper and pencil
Ruler • Scissors
Calico • Hessian (jute)
Pre-washed woollen blanket
Photocopy of sunflower
templates (see page 115)
Fusible bonding • Iron
Felt and fabric scraps
Stranded embroidery
cotton (floss)
Embroidery needle
Sewing thread and pins
Pinking shears (optional)

1 On a sheet of paper, draw a rectangle the size you want the central panel of the mat. For each place mat, use the pattern to cut one rectangle of calico; cut one from hessian (jute), adding a 2cm (3/4in) border, and one from blanket, adding a 3cm (11/4in) border.

2 To create your design, cut around the photocopied templates, arrange them on the paper pattern and draw some extra shapes such as squares and triangles. Trace all the shapes onto fusible bonding, iron the bonding onto the wrong side of felt and fabric scraps and cut out the shapes. Peel away the backing and arrange the fabric shapes on the calico. Now iron them in place and hand stitch around each shape in stranded cotton (floss) for decoration.

3 To finish, lay the appliquéd calico rectangle right side up over the hessian (jute) and machine stitch 1cm (1/2in) from each edge. Lay this right side up over the blanket and machine stitch 1.5cm (5/8in) from each edge. Finish the outer edges of the calico and hessian (jute) by teasing out the threads to fray the edges. Neaten the edges of the blanket with pinking shears, if you have them.

Flowerpot flowers

♥

WHAT YOU NEED:

Fusible bonding
Iron • Felt
Scissors • Thin stick
Stranded embroidery
cotton (floss)
Embroidery needle
Buttons • Flowerpot

1 Use the templates on page 115 to trace a flower shape and flower centre onto fusible bonding. Iron the fusible bonding onto felt scraps, cut out the shapes and peel away the backing.

2 Cut a large piece of felt for the flower back and place the end of a thin stick between both layers. Iron to fuse the two layers together and to keep the stick in place. Iron on the flower centre, then trim the excess fabric around the flower. To finish, hand stitch around the flower and centre in stranded cotton (floss), then stitch buttons at the centre. Plant the flower in a pot.

Patchwork oven gloves and pot holder

♥

WHAT YOU NEED:

Tape measure
Paper and pencil
Ruler • Scissors
Patchwork fabric (see
page 15
Pre-washed woollen blanket
or wadding (batting)
Cotton fabric
Sewing thread and pins
Decorative bias binding

1 Make a paper pattern for the oven gloves by drawing round an existing pair. Alternatively, draw an 80 x 18cm (31½ x 7in) rectangle. Mark a line 18cm (7in) up from each end for the pockets, then draw a curved line at each end to shape the pattern. Lay a piece of paper over the pattern and trace off the pocket shape.

2 Cut one oven glove and two pockets from patchwork fabric, contrasting cotton fabric and blanket or wadding (batting). With right sides facing outwards, sandwich the blanket or wadding (batting) between the two fabric layers to make one oven glove and two pocket pieces. Pin and tack (baste) around each piece.

3 To make the oven gloves, bind the top straight edge of each pocket piece with decorative bias binding (see page 17). Then lay a pocket over each end of the oven glove piece, with the patchwork fabric facing outwards. Pin, tack (baste) and stitch around the curved edges, then finish the whole outside edge of the oven glove with decorative bias binding.

4 To make the pot holder, cut a 20cm (8in) square of patchwork fabric, blanket or wadding (batting) and contrasting cotton fabric. With right sides facing outwards, sandwich the blanket or wadding (batting) between the two fabric layers. Pin and tack (baste) all three layers together. To finish, stitch decorative bias binding around the outer edge and make a hanging loop.

Carrier-bag holder

WHAT YOU NEED:

Scissors • Tape measure

Cotton fabric

Photocopy of sunflower and

leaf templates (see

page 115)

Fusible bonding

Iron • Felt scraps

Sewing thread and pins

Calico • Fabric marker pen

Stranded embroidery

cotton (floss)

Embroidery needle

Elastic • Cord

1 Cut a 35 x 48cm (13³/4 x 19in) piece of cotton fabric. Find the centre line by folding the fabric in half so that both short edges meet. Mark the fold line (centre) with tacking (basting) stitches.

2 Trace two flower shapes, two flower centres and four leaves onto fusible bonding. Iron the fusible bonding onto the wrong side of felt scraps, cut out the shapes, peel away the backing and arrange the shapes along the tacked (basted) line. Iron the shapes in place, then secure them with machine stitching. Cut a small calico patch and write 'Bags' on it using a fabric marker pen. Iron the patch on the wrong side to fix it, then use stranded cotton (floss) and running stitch to attach the patch below the flowers. Fray the edges by teasing out the threads with your fingers or a needle.

3 With right sides facing, bring the short edges of the cotton fabric together. Pin and stitch the seam, stopping 3cm (1¹/4in) from each end. Stitch a 2cm (³/4in) hem on the other two edges. To finish, thread elastic through the bottom hem, and a drawstring cord through the top one.

Sunflower banner

WHAT YOU NEED:

Hessian (jute) • Scissors

Dressmaker's chalk pencil

Narrow fabric strips

Large-eyed needle

Small buttons

Stranded embroidery cotton

(floss) or wool (yarn)

Embroidery needle

Felt scraps

Fusible bonding • Iron

Pre-washed woollen blanket

Stick

Pinking shears (optional)

1 Cut a square of hessian (jute), and use a chalk pencil to draw a large circle at the centre, with a smaller circle inside. For the petals, work large stitches of cloth strips or ribbon between the chalk circle lines using the large-eyed needle, then stitch small buttons at the centre of the flower to fill the smaller circle.

2 Use the chalk pencil to write 'Sunshine' above and 'Sunflower' below the flower, then use stranded cotton (floss) or wool (yarn) to work the letters in backstitch. Cut out and appliqué a small felt heart in each corner with a button at the centre, then work a cross-stitched border all around the design. (You'll find a template for a heart on page 118 or you can design your own.)

3 Lay the completed design right side up over a piece of woollen blanket. Stitch it in place, then cut away excess fabric (with pinking shears, if you have them), leaving a border. Finish the outer edges of the hessian (jute) by teasing out the threads to fray them. Stitch two hanging loops along the top edge, then thread a stick through the loops to hang the banner.

Easter bunnies

A cheeky little bunny pops up his head from among the long grasses to see what's going on and is captured in action on a drawstring bag, a matching card and badge. Use calico, pale cotton or light-brown felt for the bunny, a dark colour for his nose and brown or green for the grass. Fill the bag with goodies like chocolate eggs and small toys to make a welcome Easter gift for a child.

❤

WHAT YOU NEED:

Rectangle of card (A4 size is ideal) • Scissors
Calico • Pencil
Fusible bonding • Iron
Felt and fabric scraps
Stranded embroidery cotton (floss)
Embroidery needle
Calico-coloured sewing thread

Easter bunny card

1 Fold the card in half so the short edges meet. Cut a piece of calico slightly smaller than the top layer of card.
2 Trace the bunny, nose, eyes and grass shapes from page 115 onto fusible bonding. Iron the fusible bonding onto the wrong side of the felt and fabric scraps, cut out the shapes, peel away the backing and arrange the fabric shapes on the calico. Iron them in place and hand stitch around each shape with embroidery cotton (floss) for decoration. Work long straight stitches for the bunny's whiskers.
3 Lay the appliquéd calico rectangle right side up over the card and machine stitch in place 1cm (1/2in) from each edge. Finish the outer edges of the calico by teasing out the threads with your fingers or a needle to fray them.

❤

WHAT YOU NEED:

Photocopy of bunny templates (see page 115)
Fusible bonding • Iron
Felt scraps
Scissors • Card
Sewing thread
Brown fabric marker pen
Safety pin

Bunny badge

1 Trace the bunny and grass shapes from your photocopy onto fusible bonding. Iron the fusible bonding onto felt scraps, cut out the shapes and peel away the backing. Arrange the fabric shapes on the card, iron them in place, then cut out roughly.
2 Take a large felt scrap backed with fusible bonding and fuse it to the back of the card, sandwiching the card between the two layers of felt. Machine stitch around the badge shape then cut away excess card and felt. Mark the eyes, nose and whiskers with the fabric marker pen, then securely hand stitch a safety pin to the back of the badge to finish.

Draw-string bag

♥

WHAT YOU NEED:

Scissors • Tape measure
Gingham
Felt and fabric scraps
Photocopy of bunny
templates (see page 115)
Pencil
Fusible bonding • Iron
Sewing thread and pins
Two small buttons
Stranded embroidery cotton
(floss)
Embroidery needle

1 Cut a 28 x 75cm (11 x 29½in) rectangle of gingham fabric. With wrong sides facing, fold the fabric in half so both short edges meet. Arrange the fabric so the fold is at the bottom. For the drawstring channels cut two 5 x 26cm (2 x 10¼in) strips from contrasting fabric; cut two 5 x 56cm (2 x 22in) strips for the drawstrings.

2 Trace the photocopied bunny, nose and grass onto fusible bonding. Iron the bonding onto the wrong side of the felt and fabric scraps, cut out the shapes and fuse them in place; secure with machine stitching. Next stitch on the button eyes and use embroidery cotton (floss) to work long straight stitches for whiskers.

3 Press a 1cm (½in) turning round each channel strip. With right sides up, centre one strip over the gingham, 6cm (2¼in) from each short edge. Tack (baste) the strips in place and stitch just inside the long edges, leaving the short ends open.

4 With right sides facing, fold the gingham in half and stitch the two side seams, taking a 1.5cm (⅝in) seam allowance. Turn the bag out, then stitch a 1.5cm (⅝in) hem along the top edge.

5 Press a 1cm (½in) hem along each long edge of the drawstrings, then press them in half so the folds meet and stitch along the length. Thread each drawstring through both channels and knot the ends.

Just 'purrfect'

*T*hese crazy cats are just 'purrfect' to have around the house, and although they may look a bit bewildered, they will soon settle into their new home. Simple sewing techniques combined with appliqué, embroidery and fabric markers are used to make the cat collection – a doorstop, stuffed toy, juggling cats, picture and fridge magnet. Calico, felt scraps and a fabric marker pen are all you need for the stuffed toy and fridge magnet, and the picture is made from felt and fabric scraps, including an old tartan shirt for the background. An old coat forms the base fabric for the doorstop, with a combination of felt scraps, odd buttons and stranded embroidery thread (floss) for the features.

Doorstop

WHAT YOU NEED:

*Photocopy of large cat
template (see page 116)*

Scissors

*Pre-washed woollen fabric
or blanket*

Fusible bonding • Iron

Felt scraps

*Stranded embroidery
cotton (floss)*

Embroidery needle

Two small buttons

Sewing thread and pins

Polyester wadding (batting)

Old sock

Rice or kitty litter

1 Cut out the photocopy of the large cat template, omitting the extended tail, and use this as a pattern to cut out two cat shapes from the woollen fabric – one for the front and one for the back.

2 Trace the ears, tail, nose and heart shapes onto fusible bonding. Iron the bonding onto the wrong side of the felt scraps and cut out the shapes. Peel away the backing and arrange the felt shapes on the woollen front. Iron them in place. Using embroidery cotton (floss) in a contrasting colour, work blanket stitch around the heart and running stitch around the remaining shapes. Also use stranded cotton to stitch the mouth and whiskers with straight stitch and to attach the buttons for eyes. (See pages 10-11 for details on working embroidery stitches.)

3 Pin the front and back pieces together with right sides out. Tack (baste) all round the outer edges, taking a 6mm (1/4in) seam allowance and leaving a 15cm (6in) gap at the bottom. Use stranded cotton (floss) to work running stitches along the tacked (basted) line.

4 Stuff the cat shape with polyester wadding (batting) through the gap at the bottom, leaving the ears and bottom unstuffed. Fill an old sock with rice or kitty litter, then tie a knot in the end. Insert the filed sock through the gap at the bottom to add weight to the doorstop, then secure the gap by completing the line of running stitches around the edge in stranded cotton (floss).

Juggling cats

WHAT YOU NEED:

Paper and pencil

Scissors

Cotton fabric

Fusible bonding

Iron • Felt scraps

Fabric marker pen

Sewing thread and pins

Dried beans or pulses

1 Trace the medium-sized cat template from page 116, omitting the tail, then cut around your tracing to make a pattern. For each juggling cat use your pattern to cut two cat pieces from cotton fabric – one for the front and one for the back.

2 Trace the nose and heart shapes onto fusible bonding. Iron the bonding onto the felt scraps and cut out the shapes. Peel away the backing, arrange the felt shapes on the cat front and iron them in place. Use a fabric marker pen to draw in the eyes, mouth and whiskers, then press the fabric from the wrong side to fix it.

3 To make each juggling cat, place the front and back pieces together with right sides facing. Pin and machine stitch around the edges, leaving a gap at the bottom for turning. Clip the seam allowances where necessary for ease, then turn right sides out. Fill the cat with dried beans or pulses, then secure the gap with small stitches.

Calico cat

♥

WHAT YOU NEED:

*Paper and pencil
Scissors • Calico
Fabric marker pen
Fusible bonding
Iron • Felt scraps
Sewing thread and pins
Polyester wadding (batting)*

1 Trace the large cat template from page 116 and use it as a pattern to cut out two cat shapes from calico – one for the front and one for the back. Lay the calico front right side up over the traced pattern. Use the fabric marker pen to trace the eyes, mouth, whiskers and tail tip onto the calico, then press the fabric from the wrong side to fix it. (If you can't see the pattern through the calico, press the pattern and fabric up against a sunny window so it's easier to see.)

2 Trace the nose and heart shape onto fusible bonding. Iron the bonding onto the felt scraps and cut out the shapes. Peel away the backing and arrange the felt shapes on the calico cat front. Iron them in place, then stitch around each shape by hand or machine.

3 Place the front and back pieces together with right sides facing. Pin and machine stitch around the edges, taking a 6mm (1/4in) seam allowance and leaving a 10cm (4in) gap at the bottom for turning. Clip the seam allowances for ease around curves and angles, then turn the toy right sides out.

4 Lightly stuff the body and tail tip with polyester wadding (batting), leaving the ears and the rest of the tail unstuffed. Secure the gap with small stitches. Work a row of hand or machine stitches along the base of each ear and the tip and base of the tail to keep the polyester wadding (batting) in place.

Cat picture

WHAT YOU NEED:

Picture frame • Scissors
Cotton fabric for
the background
Fusible bonding • Pencil
Photocopies of cat and heart
templates in various sizes
(see page 116)
Fabric and felt scraps
Iron • Sewing thread
Fabric marker pen
Stranded embroidery
cotton (floss)
Embroidery needle
Button

1 Carefully remove the backing board from the picture frame and use this as a template to cut a piece of fabric and fusible bonding to the same size. This will provide the background for the picture.

2 Trace a large heart, the cat in two sizes, with and without tails, and the appropriate number of ears, noses, hearts and tail tips onto fusible bonding. Iron the bonding onto the wrong side of the felt and fabric scraps and cut out the shapes. Peel away the backing and arrange the fabric shapes on the base fabric. Iron them to fuse them in place, then stitch around each shape in a contrasting colour by hand or machine.

3 Mark the eyes, mouth and whiskers of the light coloured cats with a fabric marker pen. For the darker cats embroider these details with contrasting embroidery cotton, using straight stitch for the mouth and whiskers and a cross stitch for each eye. (See pages 10-11 for details on working embroidery stitches.) Work a large cross stitch in the centre of each cat's heart. Stitch a button onto the large heart for decoration.

4 To finish the picture, iron the bonding onto the wrong side of the base fabric, peel away the backing and lay the fabric over the backing board. Iron in place, then mount the picture in the frame.

Fridge magnet

WHAT YOU NEED:

Fusible bonding • Iron
Calico • Card
Fabric marker pen
Sewing thread • Ribbon
Wadding (batting)
Magnet
Multi-purpose glue

1 Trace the small cat from page 116 onto fusible bonding. Iron the bonding onto calico, cut out the shape and peel away the backing. Place the shape on the card, iron it in place, then cut out roughly. Fuse a calico scrap backed with fusible bonding to the back of the card. Stitch around the cat then cut away excess card and fabric.

2 Mark the eyes, nose, mouth and whiskers with a fabric marker pen. Stitch a ribbon bow under the mouth and a short length of ribbon to the back of the cat to hang it from.

3 Cut two 9cm (3½in) squares of calico and one of wadding (batting). Place both calico shapes over the wadding (batting), pin and machine stitch around the edges, leaving a gap for turning. Turn right sides out and secure the gap with small stitches.

4 On the front of the square use a fabric marker pen to write 'I' and 'CATS' and to put a small heart between the two using the pen or with appliqué. Add a line of crosses all round the square. Glue a magnet to the back, then stitch the ribbon with the hanging cat to the back of the fridge magnet.

Wash-day blues

Chase away your wash-day blues with these matching peg and laundry bags in brightly coloured fabrics. The bags are made from sturdy striped cotton fabric and decorated with a cord washing line and appliquéd washing. A friendly sun beams down on the washing made from a circle of embroidered felt with a button decoration. The finished bags are slipped over coat hangers so they can be hung anywhere, and will prove to be a practical addition to any household.

Laundry bag

♥

WHAT YOU NEED:

Paper and pencil
Strong coat hanger
Ruler • Scissors
Striped cotton base fabric
Cotton lining
Dressmaker's chalk pencil
Fusible bonding
Felt and fabric scraps • Iron
Sewing thread and pins
Piping cord • Three buttons
Stranded embroidery
cotton (floss)
Embroidery needle
Calico • Fabric marker pen

1 Measure the width of the coat hanger, add 2cm (³/4in) to this measurement, then draw a rectangle on the paper equal to this width and 62cm (24½in) long. For the opening, draw a large oval shape centrally 5cm (2in) from one short edge with the chalk pencil. (You may find it easiest to draw around a small oval serving dish, if you have one.) Place the coat hanger along the top of this short edge, then draw around the curved shape and mark the position of the hook. Add a 1.5cm (⁵/8in) seam allowance all the way round. Cut out the oval for the opening.

2 Follow steps 2-6 for the peg bag, overleaf, to assemble the bag but add some extra washing so you have two shirts, one pair of trousers and four socks. Stitch a button to each end of the washing line and write 'LAUNDRY' on the calico rectangle instead of 'PEGS'.

Peg bag

♥

WHAT YOU NEED:

Paper and pencil

Coat hanger • Ruler

Saucer • Scissors

Striped cotton base fabric

Cotton lining

Dressmaker's chalk pencil

Fusible bonding

Felt and fabric scraps

Iron

Sewing thread and pins

Piping cord

Button for the sun

Stranded embroidery

cotton (floss)

Embroidery needle

Calico

Fabric marker pen

1 To make a paper pattern for the peg bag, measure the width of the coat hanger, add 2cm (³/4in) to this measurement, then draw a rectangle equal to this width and 42cm (16¹/2in) long. For the opening, place a saucer centrally 5cm (2in) from one short edge, then draw around it (fig. 22). Place the coat hanger along the top of this short edge, then draw around the curved shape and mark the position of the hook. Add a 1.5cm (⁵/8in) seam allowance all the way round the pattern. Cut out the circle for the opening.

2 Cut the pattern twice from striped cotton fabric without cutting out the hole – one for the front and one for the back. Make sure the stripes run the same way on both pieces. Cut a third piece from cotton lining. Pin the striped front to the lining piece with right sides facing. Lay the pattern on top and use a chalk pencil to draw the opening on the lining; remove the pattern. Machine stitch round the line, then cut the fabric away from the centre, 1.5cm (⁵/8in) from the stitching line. Clip into the seam allowances for ease, then turn the lining through the hole to the wrong side. Press, then topstitch around the edge of the hole.

3 Trace one shirt, one pair of trousers and two socks from page 115 onto fusible bonding. Iron the bonding onto the wrong side of fabric scraps and cut out the shapes. Peel away the backing and arrange the shapes on the striped front. Iron the shapes to fuse them in place, then secure them with machine or hand stitching.

4 Stitch a length of piping cord, knotted at each end, above the washing, then stitch on a circle of felt for the sun, slightly larger than your button. Stitch the button to the centre of the circle, then use embroidery cotton (floss) and straight stitch (see page 11) to add the sun's rays and the pegs holding the washing on the line.

5 Cut a small calico patch and write 'PEGS' on it using a fabric marker pen. Iron the patch on the wrong side to fix the writing, then machine stitch it to the striped front about 1cm (³/8in) from the edges. Tease out the threads on the edges of the calico to fray them.

6 Pin, then tack the front and back bag pieces together with right sides facing. Stitch around all four edges taking a 1.5cm (⁵/8in) seam allowance and leaving a 2.5cm (1in) gap at the top for the hook of the coat hanger. Trim the seam allowances at the corners. Turn the bag right sides out and insert the coat hanger through the opening. Fill the bag with pegs.

fig. 22 Tracing the shape

Home sweet home

'Home is where the heart is,' and these projects combine the motifs of home and heart. Made in striped and floral fabrics in soft shades, the set is pretty enough to grace any home. The same templates, enlarged to different sizes, are used throughout. Fabric scraps, old woollen blankets, buttons and embroidery cotton (floss) are all you need to make the cushions. The door stop is simply a brick wrapped with padding and covered with fabric.

'Home Sweet Home' Cushion (page 37)

Heart cushion

♥

WHAT YOU NEED:

Square cushion pad
Tape measure • Scissors
Pre-washed woollen blanket
Fusible bonding
Iron • Fabric scraps
Stranded embroidery
cotton (floss)
Embroidery needle
Dressmaker's chalk pencil
Sewing thread and pins
Decorative 2.5cm (1in)
binding (see page 17)

1 Cut a square of pre-washed woollen blanket the size of your cushion pad, adding 2.5cm (1in) seam allowances all the way round. For the cushion back, cut two pieces of blanket, each two-thirds the size of the cushion front (see page 16).

2 Trace five medium hearts from page 118 onto fusible bonding and iron the bonding onto floral fabric scraps. Cut out the hearts, peel away the backing and arrange them on the blanket front with one about 5cm (2in) from each corner and one in the centre. Iron the hearts in place, then work running stitches (see page 11) around each one with contrasting embroidery cotton (floss).

3 Trace and cut out one medium and one small heart from page 118 to make templates. Use a chalk pencil to draw four medium hearts on the woollen front, placed centrally between the appliquéd hearts. Draw around the small heart, placing it centrally on each larger heart. Embroider these hearts in two rows of running stitch along each chalked outline using embroidery cotton (floss).

4 Hem one long edge of each of the remaining blanket rectangles. Lay the appliquéd front right side down on a flat surface. Pin the rectangles right side up on top so the raw edges match and the hemmed edges overlap in the centre.

5 Tack (baste) the layers in place, then stitch around all four edges, taking a 2.5cm (1in) seam allowance. Finish the edges with a 2.5cm (1in) wide binding (see page 17) and insert the square cushion pad.

Patchwork heart cushion

♥

WHAT YOU NEED:

Scissors
Photocopy of large heart
template (see page 118)
Patchwork fabric (see page 15)
Sewing thread and pins
Polyester wadding (batting)

1 Cut out the photocopied heart and use it as a pattern to cut two hearts from folded patchwork fabric. Pin the front and back pieces together with right sides facing and raw edge matching. Machine stitch around the edges, taking a 1.5cm (5/8in) seam allowance and leaving a small gap for turning. Clip the seam allowances on the curves and at the top point for ease, then turn the cushion right sides out.

2 Stuff the cushion with polyester wadding (batting) and close the gap by oversewing or with slipstitches. You can put the whole cushion in a washing machine for laundering.

$\mathcal{P}$earl button heart cushion

♥

WHAT YOU NEED:

Scissors

Photocopy of large heart

template (see page 118)

Pre-washed woollen blanket

Pearl buttons

Sewing thread and pins

Polyester wadding (batting)

1 Cut out the photocopied heart and use it as a pattern to cut two hearts from pre-washed woollen blanket – one for the front and one for the back. Stitch a selection of pearl buttons at random on the heart front.

2 Pin the front and back pieces together with right sides facing and raw edges matching. Machine stitch around the edges, leaving a gap for turning. Clip the seam allowances at curves and at the top point for ease, then turn the cushion right sides out. Stuff the cushion with polyester wadding (batting) and close the gap by oversewing or with slipstitches. Wash the cushion by hand when required.

'$\mathcal{H}$ome sweet home' cushion

♥

WHAT YOU NEED:

Square cushion pad

Scissors • Tape measure

Cotton base fabric

Calico • Fabric scraps

Photocopy of house templates

(see page 118)

Fusible bonding and iron

Stranded embroidery

cotton (floss)

Embroidery needle

Sewing needle and pins

Sewing thread

Buttons

1 For the cushion front cut a square of cotton base fabric the size of your cushion pad, adding 1.5cm (⅝in) seam allowances all the way round. For the cushion back, cut two pieces of cotton base fabric, each two-thirds the size of the cushion front (see page 16). Cut a calico square for the centre panel, a smaller floral square and an even smaller calico square. Press a 6mm (¼in) hem around all three smaller squares.

2 Cut around the photocopied templates, arrange them on the small calico square, then cut out some extra shapes for the patches – a striped rectangle makes a pretty wicket fence in front of the house, while two shapes in the sky suggest light and shadow. Trace all the shapes onto fusible bonding, iron the bonding onto the wrong side of fabric scraps and cut out the shapes. Peel away the backing and arrange the fabric shapes on the small calico square. Iron them to fuse them in place. Hand or machine stitch around each shape and sew on buttons for decoration – a yellow button makes a bright sun, surrounded by rays of straight stitch (see page 11).

3 Pin the appliquéd square right side up over the centre of the floral square. Tack (baste) and then oversew in place. Lay this square centrally over the large calico square, stitch in place and then lay this over the cushion front and stitch in place in the same way. Work a running-stitch border around the edges of the large calico and floral squares and add straight-stitch stars in the corners of the large calico square with embroidery cotton (floss). (See page 11 for details on working these embroidery stitches.)

4 Hem one long edge of each back piece. Complete the cushion following the instructions on page 16 for making a removable cover.

Patchwork bolster

♥

WHAT YOU NEED:

Scissors • Tape measure

Pre-washed woollen blanket

Pencil and paper

Fusible bonding • Iron

Floral fabric scraps

Stranded embroidery

cotton (floss)

Embroidery needle

Sewing thread and pins

Pinking shears (optional)

Polyester wadding (batting)

Twisted cord

1 Cut a 48 x 76cm (19 x 30in) rectangle of pre-washed woollen blanket as the base for the bolster. Draw an 11cm (4¼in) square on paper as a template for the patches and trace eight squares onto fusible bonding. Iron the bonding onto the wrong side of the floral fabric scraps and cut out the squares. Peel away the backing and arrange the fabric squares alternately, in four rows, at the centre of the blanket rectangle.

2 Iron the squares to fuse them in place, then work running stitches around each one with contrasting embroidery cotton (floss). Work a border of cross stitch (see page 10) in each of the eight blank squares using embroidery cotton (floss).

3 With right sides facing, bring the short edges of the blanket together. Pin and stitch the seam, then turn right sides out. Work a border of cross stitch along the top and bottom edges, then trim the raw edges with pinking shears, if you have them. Fill the tube with polyester wadding (batting) and tie the ends of the tube with twisted cord to hold the filling in place.

Door stop

♥

WHAT YOU NEED:

House brick • Bubblewrap

Sticky tape

Cotton base fabric

Pencil and paper

Fusible bonding • Iron

Scissors • Fabric scraps

Stranded embroidery

cotton (floss)

Embroidery needle

Buttons

Sewing thread • Pins

1 Wrap the brick with bubblewrap so all the edges are covered, then add extra layers to make a domed top. Secure with sticky tape.

2 Lay the cotton base fabric centrally over the domed top and use pins to mark the position of each top corner. Use the template on page 118 to trace the house shapes onto fusible bonding, then draw some extra shapes such as a triangle and rectangle for the patches. Iron the fusible bonding onto the fabric scraps, cut out the shapes and peel away the backing. Arrange the shapes on the cotton base fabric. Iron them to fuse them in place and hand or machine stitch around each one. Stitch on the buttons for decoration. Make a sun by stitching a button in the sky and working rays around it with straight stitch (see page 11). Finish each side with a border of running stitch (see page 11).

3 Wrap the brick like a present with the base fabric, placing the appliqué over the domed top. Trim any excess fabric, turn in the raw edges and oversew or slipstitch in place. Decorate the sides with a border of cross stitch.

Hanging hearts

1 Trace the medium-sized heart from page 118 and use it as a pattern to cut out ten fabric hearts. Pin the hearts together in pairs with right sides facing and machine stitch around the edges, leaving a gap in one side for turning. Turn the hearts right sides out, stuff with polyester wadding (batting) and close the gap with slipstitches.
2 Stitch a wooden bead between each heart to join them, then stitch a ribbon hanging loop on the back of the top heart, thread on a bead and secure with a knot.
3 Stitch a small felt shape and button onto alternate hearts, then stitch the bells to the bottom. You can easily make the hanging longer or shorter by changing the number of hearts and beads.

Key ring

1 If you wish, you can use the heart pattern to make a key ring. All you do is cut two medium hearts from blanket or felt and two smaller hearts from fabric scraps backed with fusible bonding. Fuse the small hearts to one of the larger hearts and decorate with running stitches in embroidery cotton (floss).
2 Pin the two larger hearts together with right sides out and work blanket stitches around the edges in stranded cotton (floss), leaving a small gap in one side for stuffing. Stuff the heart with polyester wadding (batting) and close the gap with more blanket stitches. (See pages 10-11 for details on working embroidery stitches.)
3 Finally, add a ribbon loop, made from a short strip of folded ribbon, to the top of the heart for hanging keys.

Tex Mex

The vivid colours and exotic images of Mexico are the subjects of these super projects. Cobalt blue, burnt orange, lime green and bright yellow fabrics mixed with felt, gingham, calico and hessian (jute) create these wonderful accessories – no office will be complete without a cactus computer cover, hanging wall tidy and cushion, and for the kitchen there's a colourful shopping bag, apron and herb bags decorated with sweetcorn and chillies. If you can't find fabrics in the right colours, don't worry. Simply gather up all your pale-coloured fabric scraps and dye them with hand or machine dyes.

♥

WHAT YOU NEED:

Scissors • Tape measure
Hessian (jute)
Fusible bonding • Iron
Felt and gingham scraps
Tapestry wool (yarn)
Embroidery needle
Sewing thread and pins

Shopping bag

1 Cut a 43 x 112cm (17 x 44in) piece of hessian (jute) for the bag and two 10 x 43cm (4 x 17in) hessian (jute) strips for the handles. Find the centre line by folding the bag fabric in half so that both short edges meet. Mark the fold line (centre) with tacking (basting) stitches. This will be the bottom of the bag.

2 Use a photocopier to enlarge the large cactus on page 118, then use it to trace four cacti onto fusible bonding. Trace four chillies and four chilli stalks (page 118) and one sweetcorn and one sweet-corn leaf (page 119) onto fusible bonding. Iron the bonding onto the wrong side of gingham and felt scraps, cut out the shapes, peel away the backing and arrange them on the hessian (jute) above the tacking (basting). Iron the shapes in place and secure them with machine stitching. Stitch rows of running stitches (see page 11) with tapestry wool (yarn) between the motifs to create a patchwork look.

3 With right sides facing, bring the short edges of the hessian (jute) together. Pin and stitch 1.5cm (5/8in) side seams. Stitch a 4cm (1 1/2in) hem at the top edge, then turn the bag right sides out.

4 To make the handles, press a 1.5cm (5/8in) turning along each long edge of the hessian (jute) strips; press each strip in half and stitch along the length. Stitch the ends to the top edges of the bag.

Sweetcorn cushion

♥

WHAT YOU NEED:

Pencil and paper • Ruler
Square cushion pad
Scissors • Bright fabrics
Photocopies of spiky cactus,
sweetcorn, small chilli, sun
and cloud templates (see
pages 118, 119 and 123)
Backing fabric
Fusible bonding • Iron
Felt and fabric scraps
Stranded embroidery
cotton (floss)
Embroidery needle
Pins • Sewing thread

1 On a piece of paper draw a square the size of your cushion pad. Divide the square into patches, with a large square at the centre, a small square at each corner, and a rectangle at each side. Use the paper pattern to cut each patch from bright fabric, adding 1.5cm (5/8in) seam allowances all the way round. For the cushion back, cut two pieces of backing fabric each two-thirds the size of the cushion front plus 1.5cm (5/8in) seam allowances all round (see page 16).

2 To create your appliquéd designs, trace two spiky cacti, the sweetcorn and sweetcorn leaf, two clouds, two suns and sun centres, four chillies and four chilli stalks onto fusible bonding and iron the bonding onto felt and fabric scraps. Cut out the shapes, peel away the backing and arrange them on each patch. Iron the shapes in place and secure them with machine stitching. Work long random straight stitches on the remaining patch using contrasting embroidery cotton (floss). Make the patchwork cushion front (see page 15), then work running stitches with stranded cotton (floss) around the edge of each patch. (See page 11 for details on working these embroidery stitches.)

3 Hem one long edge of each rectangle, then complete the cover following the instructions for making a removable cover on page 16.

Sweetcorn apron

♥

WHAT YOU NEED:

Paper and pencil
Ruler • Scissors
Calico
Photocopies of sweetcorn
and large chilli templates
(see pages 118-119)
Fusible bonding • Iron
Felt and gingham scraps
Gingham binding (see
page 17)
Sewing thread and pins

1 Make a paper pattern by drawing round an existing apron and adding 1.5cm (5/8in) seam and hem allowances. Alternatively, draw a 66 x 94cm (26 x 37in) rectangle. On one short edge, mark a point 15cm (6in) in from each end. On each long edge, mark a point 23cm (9in) down from the top short edge, then draw a curved line to join each side point to the point on the top short edge.

2 Cut the apron from calico and cut three 8 x 61cm (3¼ x 24in) calico strips for the ties and neck band. Trace one sweetcorn and one sweetcorn leaf, five chillies and five chilli stalks onto fusible bonding. Iron the bonding onto the wrong side of felt and gingham scraps, cut out the shapes, peel away the backing and arrange them on the apron. Iron in place, then secure with machine stitching.

3 To finish, bind the top straight edge with 3cm (1¼in) gingham binding (see page 17), then stitch a 1.5cm (5/8in) turning along the remaining edges. Press a 1.5cm (5/8in) turning along each long edge of each tie strip; press in half and stitch along the length. Stitch one strip to the top corners and the others to the apron sides.

Hanging herb bags

Bright fabric
Calico • Scissors
Photocopy of chosen template
(see pages 112-126)
Fusible bonding
Felt scraps • Iron
Sewing thread and pins
Stranded embroidery
cotton (floss)
Dried herbs • Cord
Flat braid for hanging

1 For each bag cut a 9 x 24cm (3½ x 9½in) rectangle of bright fabric. (You can make a larger or smaller bag if you wish.) Fold the fabric in half so both short edges meet. The fold is the bottom of the bag. Cut a calico patch to fit on the folded fabric then trace one of the templates onto fusible bonding. Fuse the bonding onto felt, cut out the shape and fuse it onto the patch; embroider it as desired. Machine stitch the decorative patch to the front of the bag and tease away the threads to fray the edges.

2 To assemble the bag, bring the short edges of the bag together with right sides facing, then pin and stitch 6mm (¼in) side seams. Stitch a 6mm (¼in) hem at the top edge, then turn the bag right sides out. Fill with dried herbs and tie with a cord. If you wish, make several bags and sew them onto a piece of braid, making a loop at the top for hanging.

Computer cover

Pencil and paper
Tape measure • Scissors
Blue base fabric
Sewing thread and pins
Felt and fabric scraps
Copies of cacti templates,
sun and cloud (see pages
119 and 123)
Fusible bonding • Iron
Decorative bias binding
(see page 17)

1 Measure the height and width of the monitor and draw a box to these measurements on paper, rounding off the top two corners. Add 1.5cm (⅝in) seam allowances all the way round. Use the pattern to cut two shapes from the base fabric – one for the front and one for the back. For the gusset (sides and top), measure the depth of the monitor and add 3cm (1¼in) for seam allowances. Cut a strip of base fabric this wide by the total measurement of both sides and the top of the front piece.

2 Use the paper pattern to work out the design for the cover front. Draw diagonal and horizontal lines to split the pattern into three areas suggesting the rugged landscape – blue, orange and green. Redraw the shapes, adding 1.5cm (⅝in) seam allowances to the new diagonal and horizontal lines, then cut out the pieces from fabric. Stitch them together with right sides facing and press the seams open. Pin this piece right side up over the front piece, then tack (baste) the layers together.

3 Trace the large cactus, small cactus and earth, two spiky cacti, the cloud and the enlarged sun and sun centre onto fusible bonding. Iron the bonding onto the wrong side of contrasting felt scraps and cut out the shapes. Peel away the backing and arrange the fabric shapes on the patchwork cover front. Iron them to fuse them in place, then secure the shapes with machine stitching.

4 To assemble the cover, pin the front to the gusset with right sides facing around the side and top edges, snipping into the seam allowance of the gusset piece at the corners of the front piece for ease. Tack (baste) and stitch in place. Repeat to join the other long edge of the gusset to the back piece. Turn the cover right sides out and finish the lower raw edge with decorative bias binding.

Hanging tidy

♥

WHAT YOU NEED:

Tape measure • Scissors
Hessian (jute) base fabric
Backing fabric
Bright fabrics
Fusible bonding
Iron • Felt scraps
Sewing needle and pins
Stranded embroidery
cotton (floss)
Bulldog clips • Thread
Hanging stick

1 Cut one 54 x 62cm (21¹/₄ x 24¹/₂in) rectangle from hessian (jute) and one from backing fabric. From the bright fabrics, cut three 16 x 23cm (6¹/₄ x 9in) pockets and six 9 x 15cm (3¹/₂ x 6in) loop strips.

2 To make each pocket, press a 2.5cm (1in) turning to the right side along the long top edge, machine stitch 1cm (³/₈in) from the top, then fray the edge by teasing out the threads. Press 1.5cm (⁵/₈in) to the wrong side along the other three edges.

3 Trace two spiky cacti and the cloud (see pages 119 and 123) onto fusible bonding. Iron the bonding onto felt scraps, cut out the shapes, peel away the backing and fuse them in place; secure them with machine stitching. On the blank pocket, stitch long straight stitches at random using embroidery cotton (floss).

4 Arrange the pockets in a column on the right-hand side of the hessian (jute), 7cm (2³/₄in) from the top edge, and 2.5cm (1in) from the side and bottom edges. Pin, tack (baste) and stitch the pockets in place along the side and bottom edges.

5 Trace the large cactus, small cactus, earth, sun and sun centre (see pages 119 and 123) onto fusible bonding. Iron the bonding onto felt scraps, cut out the shapes, peel away the backing and arrange the felt shapes on the hessian (jute). Iron the shapes in place and secure with machine or hand stitching.

6 Fold the strips in half with right sides facing so the long edges meet. Pin and stitch along the edge taking a 1cm (³/₈in) seam allowance, turn right sides out and arrange the seam so it runs down the centre; press. Fold the loops in half with the seams on the inside so the short edges meet, then pin to the top edge of the hessian (jute) with right sides facing and raw edges matching.

7 With right sides together, pin, tack (baste) and stitch the hessian (jute) and backing fabric together, leaving a gap along a side or lower edge for turning (see fig. 23). Snip off the seam allowances at the corners for ease, turn right sides out, close the gap by over-sewing and press. Stitch the bulldog clips to the front of the hanging tidy, then thread a stick through the loops and hang in place.

fig. 23 Stitching the hanging

Celebration

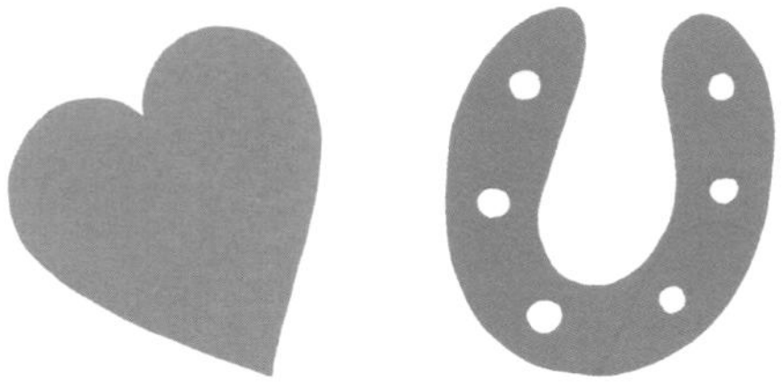

Make cards, invitations and keepsakes to celebrate special occasions like birthdays and weddings using the pretty motifs given here, or adapt your favourite motifs from the back of the book to make your own cards – you might like to make a black cat card to wish someone good luck, for example, or use the 'home sweet home' house to let people know you are moving. With a little imagination, the possibilities are endless. Use bright colours for birthdays and parties, or subtle pastels for weddings. The padded horseshoe, heart and cat make a good-luck keepsake for a bride and the motifs are repeated on the appliquéd picture to celebrate the special day.

Good-luck keepsakes

WHAT YOU NEED:

Paper and pencil • Scissors
Felt • Buttons
Stranded embroidery
cotton (floss)
Metallic embroidery thread
Embroidery needle
Polyester wadding (batting)
Dried lavender (optional)
Ribbons

1 Trace the medium-sized cat from page 116, the large horseshoe from page 117 or the medium-sized heart from page 118 onto paper. Cut out the pattern and use it to cut two shapes of felt – one for the front and one for the back. Stitch buttons onto the front of the horseshoe or heart and appliqué the small heart and nose on the cat using metallic thread; stitch the cat's mouth with straight stitch and use buttons, beads or embroidery for the cat's eyes.

2 Pin the front to the back with right sides out and stitch together around the edges with blanket stitch (see page 10) using metallic embroidery thread. Stop before you get all the way around so you can fill the shape with wadding (batting) and dried lavender (if you have some). Complete the blanket stitching then attach a ribbon for hanging the keepsake.

Wedding picture

WHAT YOU NEED:

Picture frame • Scissors
Cotton fabric for backing
Wadding (batting)
Fusible bonding
Dressmaker's chalk pencil
Iron • Pencil
Felt and fabric scraps
Stranded embroidery cotton
(floss) or metallic thread
Embroidery needle
Sewing thread (optional)
Buttons and beads (optional)

1 Carefully remove the backing board from the picture frame and use this as a template to cut one rectangle of cotton fabric as the base fabric for your picture, one rectangle of wadding (batting) and two rectangles of fusible bonding. Draw lines with a chalk pencil on the right side of the base fabric to divide it into the sections shown in the picture (page 47). Briefly place the frame on top so you can mark which areas will show when the picture is framed.

2 Trace one small cat from page 116, two small horseshoes from page 117, four small hearts from page 118 and one even smaller heart from page 117 onto fusible bonding. Cut a rectangle of fusible bonding which will fit in the centre panel of the picture. Iron the bonding onto the wrong side of the felt and fabric scraps and cut out the shapes. Peel away the backing and arrange the fabric shapes in the sections on the base fabric; iron them to fuse them in place.

3 Hand or machine stitch around each shape in contrasting or metallic thread and use straight or blanket stitches around the rectangle. Embroider the features on the cat in running stitch and straight stitch and work cross stitches on the horseshoes. (See pages 10-11 for details on working embroidery stitches.)

4 Use the chalk pencil to write the names of the happy couple on the bonded rectangle, and the date of the wedding with two small hearts in another section; add the words 'Love', 'Luck' and 'Happiness' to the remaining sections. Work the words and hearts in backstitch using embroidery cotton (floss), then work a border in cross stitch around each section.

5 To finish, iron one rectangle of fusible bonding onto the wrong side of the appliquéd picture. Peel away the backing and lay the picture right side up over the wadding (batting). Place a cloth over the picture and press carefully to bond it to the wadding. Fuse the remaining fusible bonding to the back of the wadding (batting), then bond this to the backing board with the picture on top. Insert the picture in the frame and secure it.

Cards and invitations

WHAT YOU NEED:

*Card rectangle (A4 size
is ideal)*

Scissors • Backing fabric

Felt tip or pencil

Fusible bonding • Iron

Felt scraps

Fabric marker pen (optional)

Lace or ricrac braid scraps

Buttons (optional)

Sewing thread

*Stranded embroidery
cotton (floss)*

Embroidery needle

*Multi-purpose glue
(optional)*

1 Fold the card in half so the short edges meet. Cut a piece of backing fabric slightly smaller than the folded card.

2 Trace the celebration templates you require from pages 116-117 onto fusible bonding, enlarging them as required on a photocopier beforehand. Iron the fusible bonding onto the wrong side of the felt scraps, cut out the shapes, peel away the backing and arrange the fabric shapes on the backing fabric. Iron the shapes to fuse them in place, then use machine or hand stitching to secure them. Do the same with any letters you wish to add, but omit the stitching or write the letters on with the marker pen.

3 Stitch on a border of lace, ricrac or other braid if you intend to fray the edges of the base fabric and add more braid or lace to the design as required. Add buttons and any other decorations you like.

4 Lay the appliquéd fabric, right side up, over the card and machine stitch 1cm (¹/₂in) from each edge of the fabric. Finish the outer edges of the backing fabric by teasing out the threads to fray them. Alternatively, stitch the fabric to the card, trim the edges close to the stitching and glue braid on top to cover the edges. Write your message inside the card.

Fruit picnic set

There's nothing more enjoyable than a picnic on a lazy summer day, and to make it even more fun, here's a picnic set decorated in bright colours and fresh fruit motifs. The focus of the set is a crisp cloth, beautifully embroidered with a ripe pineapple, watermelon slices and bunches of grapes. The comfortable cushion is appliquéd with watermelon slices, and to complete the set there's a bottle bag appropriately decorated with a bunch of grapes. You shouldn't need to buy many materials to make the set – the cloth and cushion shown are based on an old linen sheet, the cushion borders were once a child's pair of trousers, and the grapes on the bottle bag are odd buttons.

Fruit tablecloth

♥

WHAT YOU NEED:

*Tablecloth, sheet or
large square of cotton or
linen fabric
Dressmaker's chalk pencil
Ruler
Stranded embroidery cotton
(floss) in several colours
Embroidery needle*

1 Use a tablecloth or cut a sheet or piece of cotton or linen fabric to the required size. Enlarge the fruit on page 121 on a photocopier or using the grid method (see page 8). Lay the fabric right side up over the photocopied design and use a chalk pencil to trace around the design. Using a ruler to help you, draw the position of a border an equal distance from each edge.

2 Embroider the outlines of each fruit and the border with 1-3 rows of large, parallel running stitches (see page 11), using embroidery cotton (floss). Unless you are using a tablecloth, finish the edges by teasing out the threads to fray them.

Melon cushion

♥

WHAT YOU NEED:

*Pencil and paper
Square cushion pad
Scissors
Felt and fabric scraps
Cotton fabric for the
cushion back
Fusible bonding • Iron
Sewing thread and pins
Stranded embroidery
cotton (floss)
Embroidery needle
Buttons • Sewing thread*

1 On a piece of paper draw a square the size of your cushion pad. Divide the square into patches, with a large square at the centre, a small square at each corner and a rectangle at each side. Cut each patch from fabric, adding 1.5cm (⅝in) seam allowances all the way round. For the cushion back, cut two pieces of cotton fabric, each two-thirds the size of the cushion front, plus 1.5cm (⅝in) seam allowances all round (see page 16).

2 Trace the melon shapes from page 121 (enlarging them, if required) twice onto fusible bonding and iron the bonding onto the wrong side of felt and fabric scraps. Cut out the shapes, peel away the backing and arrange the shapes on the centre patch. Iron them in place and secure with machine stitching. Work blanket stitch (see page 10) along the cut edge of the melon slices using embroidery cotton (floss) and add buttons for pips.

3 Assemble the patchwork cushion front (see page 15), then work running stitches around each corner patch with embroidery cotton (floss).

4 Hem one long edge of each fabric rectangle for the cushion back. Lay the cushion front on a flat surface, right side up and pin the back pieces right sides down on top, with the raw edges matching and the hemmed edges overlapping at the centre.

5 Tack (baste) the layers together, then stitch around all four edges taking a 1.5cm (⅝in) seam allowance. Trim the seam allowances at the corners for ease. Turn the cover right sides out and insert the cushion pad.

Grape bottle bag

♥

WHAT YOU NEED:

Scissors • Tape measure
Check fabric
Fusible bonding
Iron • Felt scraps
Stranded embroidery
cotton (floss)
Embroidery needle
Buttons
Fabric marker pen
Sewing thread and pins

1 From check fabric cut one 34 x 90cm (13½ x 35½in) rectangle and two 8 x 38cm (3¼ x 15in) handle strips. Fold the rectangle in half so both short edges meet. The fold is the bottom of the bag.

2 Trace two grape leaves from page 121 onto fusible bonding and iron the bonding onto felt. Cut out the shapes, peel away the backing and arrange them on the fabric rectangle above the fold. Iron the leaves in place and secure them by working a line of running stitches around the leaf edges with embroidery cotton (floss). Firmly stitch on the buttons to represent the grapes. Use a fabric marker pen to draw in leaf tendrils, then press from the wrong side to fix the pen marks.

3 With right sides facing, fold the rectangle in half so the short edges meet and the fold is at the bottom. Pin and stitch 1.5cm (⁵/₈in) side seams, then stitch a 4cm (1½in) hem at the top edge. Turn the bag right sides out.

4 For the handles, press a 1.5cm (⁵/₈in) turning along each long edge of each fabric strip, then press each strip in half and stitch along the length. Stitch the ends to the top edge of the bag.

Starlight, starbright

Your child will love going to sleep surrounded by this set of starry nursery accessories made in fresh cotton fabrics and bright felt scraps. All the items are remarkably quick and easy to stitch, so you can make the whole set in no time. Basic patchwork and appliqué techniques and a few simple embroidery stitches help to create the stunning cot cover, hanging mobile, cushions, star garland and wall plaque.

♥

WHAT YOU NEED:

Wire coat hanger
Pencil and paper • Calico
Photocopies of small moon
and both star templates
(see page 120)
Fusible bonding • Iron
Contrasting fabric scraps
Pins and sewing thread
Gingham fabric
Card • Narrow ribbon

Stars mobile

1 To make the paper pattern for the cover, lay the coat hanger on a piece of paper, draw around it and mark the position of the hook. Add 2cm (³/₄in) for ease plus a 1.5cm (⁵/₈in) seam allowance to the curved edges and 2.5cm (1in) to the bottom edge. Use this pattern to cut two pieces of calico – one for the front and one for the back.

2 Use the photocopies to trace two moons and four small stars onto fusible bonding. Iron the bonding onto the wrong side of contrasting fabric scraps and cut out the shapes. Peel away the backing and arrange one moon and two stars on each calico shape. Iron to fuse them in place, then secure the shapes with machine stitching.

3 Pin the calico shapes together with right sides facing. Tack (baste) the layers together, then stitch around the curved edges leaving a 2.5cm (1in) gap at the top for the hook of the coat hanger. Turn the cover right sides out, insert the coat hanger and bind the bottom edges together with gingham bias binding (see page 17). Make a tube of gingham fabric to cover the hook.

4 Trace as many large stars as you want onto fusible bonding. Iron the fusible bonding onto fabric scraps, cut out the stars and peel away the backing. Place the fabric stars on the card, iron in place, then cut out roughly. To finish, fuse a fabric scrap backed with fusible bonding onto the back of the card, then cut away the excess card and fabric. Attach the stars to the bound edge of the cover with lengths of narrow ribbon.

Patchwork cot cover

♥

WHAT YOU NEED:

Pencil and paper

Tape measure • Scissors

Backing fabric

Wadding (batting)

Calico for borders

Gingham and floral fabrics

Fusible bonding • Iron

Fabric marker pen

Sewing thread

Pins

Gingham binding (see page 17)

1 On paper draw a 60 x 90cm (23¹/₂ x 35¹/₂in) rectangle. Cut a piece of backing fabric and wadding (batting) to this size, adding 1.5cm (⁵/₈in) seam allowances all the way round. Draw a 10cm (4in) wide border on the paper pattern and divide the centre into sections as shown (fig. 24). Label the sections and mark the fabric to be used. On the border sections of the pattern write the lines 'Good night... zzz', 'sleep tight', 'Sweet dreams... in', 'the night.... zzz'. Cut the pattern into its sections then cut patches from appropriate fabrics, adding 1.5cm (⁵/₈in) seam allowances all the way round.

2 Use a photocopier to adjust the large star on page 120, then trace several small stars, plus the large and small moons from the same page, onto fusible bonding. Iron the bonding onto the wrong side of the fabric scraps. Cut out the shapes, peel away the backing and arrange them on the patches. Iron the shapes to fuse them in place, then secure them with machine stitching.

3 With the fabric marker pen, trace the verse onto each calico border patch, using a broken line to make the writing look like stitching. Iron the border fabrics from the wrong side to fix the marker pen. Stitch the cot cover front pieces together like a patchwork (see page 15).

4 To finish, place the backing fabric right side down, lay the wadding (batting) over it and then pin the patchwork front right side up on top so all the raw edges match. Tack (baste) and machine stitch around the edges and along the border seams, then bind the edges with gingham binding (see page 17).

fig. 24 Cot cover design

Reversible door plaque

♥

WHAT YOU NEED:

Scissors • Tape measure
Wadding (batting)
Blue and yellow
cotton fabrics • Calico
Fabric marker pens
Sewing thread
Length of piping cord

1 Cut one 15 x 26cm (6 x 10$^{1/4}$in) rectangle of wadding (batting) and one each of yellow and blue cotton fabric; cut two 8 x 19cm (3$^{1/4}$ x 7$^{1/2}$in) rectangles of calico. Use fabric marker pens to write 'Sweet Dreams' and 'zzz' and to draw a moon and stars on one calico rectangle; on the other rectangle write 'Hello Sunshine' with a sun, flowers and leaves. Press the calico shapes from the wrong side to fix the ink.

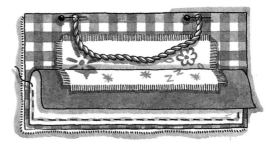

fig. 25 Stitching the plaque

2 Place the 'Hello Sunshine' rectangle centrally over the right side of the yellow fabric, and the 'Sweet Dreams' rectangle on the blue fabric. Machine stitch the calico rectangles in place 6mm ($^{1/4}$in) from the edges, then fray the edges of the calico pieces by teasing out the threads with your fingers or a needle.

3 Lay the yellow rectangle right side up over the wadding (batting) shape, then lay the cord on top with both ends level with the top fabric edge and the main part of the cord resting in a loop over the yellow fabric. Lay the blue rectangle on top, right side down (see fig. 25). Pin and machine stitch around the edges, leaving a gap in one side for turning and stitching twice over the cord for strength. Trim the seam allowances at the corners for ease, turn the plaque right sides out and machine stitch close to the edges, closing the gap as you do so.

Starlight picture

WHAT YOU NEED:

Paper and pencil • Scissors

Dark fabric • Calico

Polyester wadding (batting)

Sewing thread and pins

Fusible bonding • Iron

Fabric and felt scraps

Metallic threads

Embroidery needle

Gold marker pen

Stranded embroidery

cotton (floss)

Buttons

1 Draw your design on paper, using the picture below as your reference and tracing the stars from page 120, if desired. On the border sections write the lines 'Starlight, Starbright', 'First star I've seen tonight', 'I wish I may, I wish I might', 'Get the wish I wish tonight'. Draw a square around the design, then use this to cut out dark fabric for the picture base.

2 To make the padded base, use the template to draw another square, adding 5cm (2in) all the way round. Use this larger square as a pattern to cut two calico squares and one square of wadding (batting). Lay both calico squares over the square of wadding (batting). Pin and machine stitch around the edges, leaving a gap for turning. Turn the square right sides out, then machine stitch close to the edges, closing the gap as you do so.

3 Trace the star and triangle templates from the paper pattern onto fusible bonding. Iron the bonding onto the wrong side of the felt

and fabric scraps and cut out the shapes. Peel away the backing and arrange the fabric shapes on the base fabric. Iron to fuse them in place, then work running stitch around each one with metallic thread. Use the same thread to work long running stitches along the edge of the border.

4 Write the lines of the poem on the border with a gold marker pen, then work backstitches (see page 10) over the writing in metallic thread. Embroider small straight-stitch stars with embroidery cotton (floss) at random on the design and at each border corner, then stitch buttons onto the appliquéd stars.

5 Centre the appliquéd picture over the padded calico square and machine stitch 1cm (¹/₂in) from each edge. Finish the outer edges of the picture by teasing out the threads to fray them. Stitch a hanging loop at the back.

Star garland

WHAT YOU NEED:

Scissors • Fabric scraps
Sewing thread and pins
Polyester wadding (batting)
Wooden beads • Cord
Buttons (optional)

1 Trace the large star from page 120 and use it to cut ten fabric stars. Pin them together in pairs with right sides facing, then machine stitch around the edges, taking a narrow seam allowance and leaving a gap for turning. Clip the seam allowances where necessary for ease, then turn the stars right sides out.

2 Stuff each star with polyester wadding (batting) and close the gap with slipstitches. Join the stars into a line by stitching a wooden bead between each one. Stitch a cord hanging loop to each end star, thread a bead onto the cord, then secure it with a knot. Stitch small buttons onto alternate stars, if you wish, for added decoration.

Star cushions

WHAT YOU NEED:

Scissors
Cotton fabric
Sewing thread and pins
Polyester wadding (batting)

1 Use a photocopier or the grid method (see page 8) to enlarge the large star on page 120, then use it as a pattern to cut two stars from cotton fabric. Pin the cotton stars together with right sides facing and machine stitch around the edges, taking a 1cm (¹/₂in) seam allowance and leaving a gap for turning.

2 Clip the seam allowances where necessary for ease, then turn the cushion right sides out. Stuff the cushion with small pieces of polyester wadding (batting), then close the gap in the cushion by oversewing or with small slipstitches.

flowers and bees

Traditional English embroidery patterns with country themes were the inspiration for this group of projects featuring colourful wild flowers, honey bees and bird boxes. Old woollen blankets, odd buttons and embroidery threads are the basic materials needed to make the projects – a pin cushion, a glasses' case and matching needle case, two pretty greetings cards, a stunning waistcoat and a delightful embroidered hanging. If you don't have old blanket in a colour you like, you can easily dye it – because wool absorbs a lot of dye, you end up with soft, subtle shades. If you're short of materials to make the cards, hanging or bag, adjust their sizes accordingly.

Pin cushion

WHAT YOU NEED:

Scissors
Pre-washed woollen blanket
Calico
Dressmaker's chalk pencil
Sewing thread and needle
Buttons
Stranded embroidery cotton (floss)
Embroidery needle
Tapestry wool (yarn)
Wadding (batting)

1 Cut two 13cm (5in) squares of blanket and one 9cm (3½in) square of calico. Using the template on page 114 as your reference, draw flowers and leaves on the calico square with a dressmaker's chalk pencil. Stitch on buttons for the flower centres and work the petals and leaves in lazy-daisy stitch (see page 10) with stranded embroidery cotton (floss).

2 Pin the embroidered calico square over one of the blanket squares with right sides up. Machine stitch them together 6mm (¼in) from the edges of the calico, then tease out threads to fray the edges of the calico.

3 Pin the embroidered square right side up over the remaining blanket square. Work decorative blanket stitches (see page 10) around the edges with tapestry wool (yarn), leaving a small gap for stuffing. Fill the cushion with wadding (batting) then complete the blanket stitching.

Glasses' case

1 Cut two 13 x 22cm (5 x 8³/₄in) rectangles of pre-washed blanket and one 9 x 15cm (3¹/₂ x 6in) rectangle of calico. Using the template on page 114 as your reference, draw flowers, grass and bees on the calico rectangle with a chalk pencil. Stitch on buttons for the flower centres. Now use embroidery cotton (floss) to embroider the petals in straight stitch or lazy-daisy stitch, the grass in lazy-dazy stitch, and the stalks and bees in backstitch. (See pages 10-11 for details on working embroidery stitches.)

2 Pin the embroidered calico rectangle over one of the blanket rectangles and machine stitch together 6mm (¹/₄in) from the edges of the calico. Tease out threads to fray the edges of the calico.

3 Stitch a 1cm (¹/₂in) hem along the top (short) edge of each blanket rectangle and decorate with blanket stitch (see page 10) using tapestry wool (yarn). Pin the two rectangles together with rights sides out and hemmed edges matching, then work blanket stitches around the side and bottom edges with tapestry wool (yarn).

Needle case

1 Cut one 9cm (3¹/₂in) square of calico, one 13 x 24cm (5 x 9¹/₂in) rectangle of pre-washed blanket and two 10 x 21.5cm (4 x 8¹/₂in) rectangles of felt. Trim the edges of the felt with pinking shears, if you have them.

2 Machine stitch a 6mm (¹/₄in) turning all round the blanket rectangle, then decorate the edges with blanket stitch (see page 10) using tapestry wool (yarn). Fold the rectangle in half, right sides out, so that the short edges meet. Mark the fold line (centre) with tacking (basting) stitches.

3 Using the template on page 114 as your reference, draw flowers and leaves on the calico square with a chalk pencil. Stitch on buttons for the flower centres and work the petals and leaves in lazy-daisy stitch (see page 10) with embroidery cotton (floss).

4 Pin the embroidered calico square centrally over the front of the folded blanket. Unfold the blanket and machine stitch the square in place 6mm (¹/₄in) from the edges of the calico. Tease out threads to fray the edges of the calico.

5 Lay the blanket rectangle right side down and arrange the felt rectangles centrally on top. Pin them in place, then stitch through all three layers along the tacked (basted) line with small hand or machine stitches.

Embroidered hanging

♥

WHAT YOU NEED:

Tape measure

Scissors • Calico

Wadding (batting)

Dressmaker's chalk pencil

Sewing thread and needle

Buttons

Stranded embroidery

cotton (floss)

Embroidery needle

Stick for hanging

1 Cut two 29 x 37cm (11¹/₂ x 14¹/₂in) rectangles of calico and one of wadding, adding a 1.5cm (⁵/₈in) seam allowance all the way round each piece. Cut four 9 x 13cm (3¹/₂ x 5in) calico strips for the hanging loops.

2 Using a calico rectangle for the front, mark the position of the panels with the chalk pencil. Referring to the template on page 114, add the flowers, grass, bird houses, sun, bees and words. Stitch on buttons for the flower centres then use embroidery cotton (floss) to work the petals in straight stitch or lazy-daisy stitch, the grass in lazy-daisy stitch and the stalks, bees, words and bird houses in back-stitch. Work the panel borders with lines of cross stitch. (See pages 10-11 for details on working embroidery stitches.)

3 Fold the calico strips in half with the long edges matching and right sides facing, and stitch the long edge, taking a 1cm (¹/₂in) seam allowance. Turn the strips right sides out and centre the seam on one side; press. Work a border of cross stitch close to each edge. Fold the strips in half so the short edges meet and pin them along the top edge of the embroidered picture front so that right sides are facing and raw edges meet (see page 45, fig. 23).

4 Place the picture front right side up over the wadding (batting), then pin the other calico rectangle on top. Tack (baste) and stitch the layers together, leaving a gap in one side edge for turning. Trim the seam allowances at the corners and turn right sides out. Secure the gap by oversewing or with slipstitches then press the hanging. Thread a stick through the loops and hang on the wall.

Embroidered cards

WHAT YOU NEED:

*Card rectangle (A4 size
is ideal)* • *Scissors
Calico or hessian (jute)
Dressmaker's chalk pencil
Sewing thread and needle
Buttons* • *Stranded embroidery
cotton (floss)
Embroidery needle*

1 Fold the card in half so the short edges meet. Cut a piece of calico or hessian (jute) slightly smaller than the folded card. Using the template on page 114 as your reference, draw your chosen design on the calico/hessian (jute) rectangle with a chalk pencil. Stitch on buttons for the flower centres, then use embroidery cotton (floss) to work the petals in straight stitch or lazy-daisy stitch, the grass in lazy-daisy stitch and the stalks and bird house in backstitch. Finally, work a border of cross-stitch around the design. (See pages 10-11 for details on working embroidery stitches.)

2 Lay the embroidered fabric right side up over the card. Machine stitch 1cm (¹/₂in) from each edge of the fabric, then tease out the threads to fray the edges. Write your message inside.

Embroidered waistcoat

♥

WHAT YOU NEED:

Purchased waistcoat pattern
Pre-washed woollen blanket
Dressmaker's chalk pencil
Sewing thread and needle
Buttons • Scissors
Tapestry wool (yarn)
Embroidery needle

1 Make the waistcoat from blanket, following the pattern instructions. Using the template on page 114 as your reference, draw your design on the waistcoat fronts with a chalk pencil.

2 Stitch on buttons for the flower centres then use tapestry wool (yarn) to embroider the petals in straight stitch or lazy-daisy stitch, the grass in lazy-daisy stitch and the stalks in backstitch. (See pages 10-11 for details on working embroidery stitches.) Finish the waistcoat edges with running stitches worked in tapestry wool (yarn).

Sewing bag

♥

WHAT YOU NEED:

Scissors • Tape measure
Pre-washed woollen blanket
Hessian (jute)
Dressmaker's chalk pencil
Sewing thread and needle
Buttons
Stranded embroidery
cotton (floss)
Embroidery needle
Pins • Tapestry wool (yarn)

1 Cut a 34 x 80cm (13$^1/_2$ x 31$^1/_2$in) rectangle and two 5 x 38cm (2 x 15in) handle strips of blanket; cut one 21 x 27cm (8$^1/_4$ x 10$^3/_4$in) patch of hessian (jute).

2 Using the template on page 114 as your reference, draw flowers and grass on the hessian (jute) patch with a chalk pencil. Stitch on buttons for the flower centres, then use embroidery cotton (floss) to work the petals and grass in lazy-daisy stitch and the stalks in backstitch. Work a border of cross stitch close to the fabric edges. (See pages 10-11 for details on working embroidery stitches.)

3 Fold the blanket rectangle in half so the short edges meet. The fold is the bottom of the bag. Pin the embroidered patch centrally over the front of the folded blanket shape, unfold the fabric and machine stitch the patch in place 1.5cm (5/8in) from its edges. Tease out threads with your fingers or a needle to fray the edges.

4 Fold the blanket in half with right sides facing. Pin and stitch 1.5cm (5/8in) side seams, then stitch a 2.5cm (1in) hem at the top edge; turn the bag right sides out. For the handles, stitch a small hem on each long edge of the handle strips then stitch the ends to the top of the bag. Finish all the hemmed edges with running stitch using tapestry wool (yarn).

Nautical bathroom

Cast-off clothes and fabric scraps in red, white and blue combine to make bathroom accessories with a nautical theme – a bath mat, hanging tidy and picture. The same templates, enlarged to different sizes, are used throughout. The padded picture is made from fabric scraps, including an old pair of chef's trousers, a chef's apron forms the base fabric for the bath mat, and an old shirt makes up the striped border. The hanging tidy is adorned with felt and fabric scraps, odd buttons and piping cord.

♥

WHAT YOU NEED:

Paper and pencil
Scissors • Pins
Photocopy of cloud
(page 123)
Calico • Wadding (batting)
Fusible bonding • Iron
Felt and fabric scraps
Sewing thread
Beads • Piping cord

Padded picture

1 On a sheet of paper draw a rectangle the size you want the picture to be. Trace and cut out the boat and sea from page 122 and the photocopied cloud. Arrange them at the centre of the paper pattern and draw a small square for the sun. Draw an equal border all round the design (see page 16), then cut out the rectangle to use as a pattern. Trace the centre and border shapes on to paper and cut them out.

2 Cut one large calico rectangle for the picture back, and one of wadding (batting), one calico centre panel for the picture front, and fabric strips for the border sections, adding a 1.5cm (5/8in) seam allowance all the way round each piece.

3 Trace the design shapes onto fusible bonding, iron the bonding onto the wrong side of felt and fabric scraps and cut out the shapes. Peel away the backing and arrange the fabric shapes on the calico front. Iron them in place, then secure with machine stitching.

4 Stitch the border pieces in place (see page 16). Lay the picture right side up, over the wadding (batting), then pin the remaining calico shape on top. Tack (baste) and stitch the layers together, leaving a gap for turning. Turn right sides out and close the gap by oversewing or with slipstitches.

5 Quilt the picture border by working a row of machine stitches around the inner and outer edges. Thread beads onto a length of cord, then hand stitch along the bottom border to form loops. Finally, stitch a length of cord to the top to form a hanging loop.

Hanging tidy

♥

WHAT YOU NEED:

Tape measure • Scissors
Navy-blue base fabric
Backing fabric
Fusible bonding • Iron
Felt and fabric scraps
Sewing needle and pins
Sewing thread
Buttons • Piping cord
Stick for hanging

1 Cut one 42 x 68cm (16$^1/_2$ x 26$^3/_4$in) rectangle of base fabric and one of backing fabric. For the pockets, cut three 13cm (5in) squares and four 18cm (7in) squares of base fabric, and for the hanging loops cut four 10 x 13cm (4 x 5in) rectangles of base fabric.

2 To make the pockets, stitch a 1.5cm ($^5/_8$in) turning along the top edge, then press a 1.5cm ($^5/_8$in) turning along the remaining edges. Trace three boats from page 122 and one cloud, one sun and one sun centre from page 123 onto fusible bonding. Iron the bonding onto the wrong side of contrasting felt and fabric scraps, cut out the shapes, peel away the backing and arrange the fabric shapes on each pocket piece. Leave two pockets blank. Iron the shapes in place, then secure them with machine stitching.

3 Arrange the pockets in rows on the base fabric, with the three smaller pockets on the top row, and two rows of two larger pockets. Leave a border of 11cm (4$^1/_4$in) along the top edge and 6cm (2$^1/_4$in) around the side and bottom edges. Pin, tack (baste) and stitch the pockets in place, then add decorative buttons and piping to the blank pockets.

4 For the hanging loops, fold each rectangle in half, so the right sides are facing and the long edges meet. Pin, tack (baste) and stitch along the long edge, then turn through to the right side, centre the seam and press. Fold the loops in half so the short edges meet and the seams are on the inside. Pin to the top edge of the base fabric so the right sides are facing and the raw edges match. With right sides facing, pin, tack (baste) and stitch the base and backing fabrics together, leaving a gap for turning. Snip the seam allowances at corners for ease, then turn the hanging right side out and press it. Topstitch round the edge of the hanging. Hang from a stick.

Bath mat

♥

WHAT YOU NEED:

Paper • Pencil
Strong cotton fabric for base
and backing
Padding • Fabric scraps
Fusible bonding
Sewing thread • Ribbon

1 The bath mat is a larger version of the padded picture (page 66). Follow the instructions for the picture but enlarge the motifs on a photocopier, omit the cord and beads and add a ribbon mast.

2 Finish the mat by quilting around some of the appliquéd shapes, then work rows of machine stitches around the edges to strengthen the mat. The mat will need regular washing, so choose a strong fabric such as cotton drill for the base fabric and medium-weight cotton scraps for the motifs. Pre-wash all fabrics before use to shrink them and to make sure that colours do not run.

Funky fish

*I*f your beach or bath towels have seen better days,
don't throw them away. Instead, turn them into a
fabulous beach bag or a colourful and practical
cushion. Even old flannels can be useful – dye
them and use them to decorate the cushions. Add
appliqué details to your beach towel to tie in with
the theme, and make a colourful cotton windbreak
to complete the set. You can base the windbreak
on an old sheet, dyed blue, or buy cheap
cotton fabric for the purpose.

Windbreak

WHAT YOU NEED:

*Cotton base fabric
dyed navy blue
Backing fabric the same
width as the base fabric
Tape measure • Scissors
Pencil and paper
Fusible bonding • Iron
Fabric and felt scraps
Sewing thread • Pins
Wooden sticks (broomsticks
are ideal)
Sharp knife*

1 Cut one 1.9m (2¹/₈yd) length of base fabric and one of backing fabric. Press a 1.5cm (⁵/₈in) turning along each short edge.

2 Because the windbreak is so large, it's easiest to work out your design before cutting the shapes from fabric. First adapt the large star and both fish from pages 120 and 122 on a photocopier or using the grid system (page 8). Trace the fish and star shapes onto paper, cut them out and arrange them on the base fabric.

3 Calculate how many shapes you need, and in what sizes, then trace them onto fusible bonding. Iron the bonding onto felt and fabric scraps, cut out the shapes, peel away the backing and arrange the shapes on the base fabric. Iron the shapes to fuse them in place, then secure them with machine stitching.

4 Pin, then tack (baste) the completed base fabric over the backing fabric with right sides out so all edges match. Machine stitch the layers together along the short edges. Measure the circumference of your wooden sticks, divide by two and add 1cm (¹/₄in). Stitch two parallel rows this measurement apart at each short edge to make a channel. Stitch another parallel channel 60cm (23¹/₂in) from each short end. Stitch the layers together along both long edges, leaving the ends of each channel open.

5 Measure the height of the windbreak, add 28cm (11in) and cut four wooden sticks to this length. To make it easier to push the sticks into the sand, use a knife to sharpen one end of each stick, like a pencil. Insert the sticks into the channels along the windbreak with the pointed ends at the bottom.

Spotty starfish cushion

WHAT YOU NEED:

*Old towel pre-washed and
dyed orange
Scissors • Paper and pencil
Fusible bonding • Iron
Towelling scraps
Sewing thread and pins
Polyester wadding (batting)*

1 Use a photocopier or the grid system (see page 8) to enlarge the star on page 120, then use it as a pattern to cut two stars from towel – one for the front and one for the back. Draw a circle on paper the size you want the spots to be. Trace some spots onto paper, cut out the spots and arrange them on the star template to work out how many you need.

2 Trace the spots onto fusible bonding. Iron the bonding onto towelling scraps, cut out the shapes, peel away the backing and arrange the spots on the star front. Iron the spots to fuse them in place, then secure them with machine zigzag stitching.

3 To assemble the starfish cushion, pin the front and back pieces together with right sides facing. Machine stitch around the edges taking a 1.5cm (⅝in) seam allowance and leaving a gap for turning. Clip the seam allowances where necessary for ease, then turn the cushion right sides out. Stuff with polyester wadding (batting) and close the gap by oversewing or with slipstitches.

Fish cushion

WHAT YOU NEED:

*Old towel pre-washed
and dyed red
Scissors • Paper and pencil
Fusible bonding • Iron
Towelling scrap for the eye
Dressmaker's chalk pencil
Stranded embroidery
cotton (floss)
Embroidery needle
Sewing thread and pins
Polyester wadding (batting)*

1 Use a photocopier or the grid system (see page 8) to enlarge the large fish on page 122, then use it as a pattern to cut two fish from the towel – one for the front and one for the back.

2 Draw a circle for the eye, then trace the shape onto fusible bonding. Iron the bonding onto a towelling scrap, cut out the circle, peel away the backing and arrange the eye on the towelling fish front. Iron the circle to fuse it in place, then secure it with machine zigzag stitching. Use a chalk pencil to draw a line for the mouth, then work along the line in backstitch (see page 10) with stranded embroidery cotton (floss).

3 Pin the front and back pieces together with right sides facing. Machine stitch around the edges, taking a 1.5cm (⅝in) seam allowance and leaving a gap for turning. Clip the seam allowances where necessary for ease, then turn the cushion right sides out. Stuff with polyester wadding (batting), leaving the fins and tail unstuffed, then secure the gap by oversewing or with slipstitches. Machine stitch around each fin and the tail, then quilt them with parallel rows of stitching about 1cm (½in) apart.

Towelling beach bag

1 Cut a 7cm (2³/₄in) strip off one long length of the towel, then fold the towel in half so the short edges meet. From the towelling strip cut eight 10cm (4in) lengths for the drawstring loops.

2 It's a good idea to work out your design before you cut the shapes from fabric. Trace the photocopied shapes onto paper. Cut out the paper shapes and arrange them on the bag fabric.

3 Work out how many of each shape you need, then trace the shapes onto fusible bonding. Iron the bonding onto felt and fabric scraps, cut out the shapes, peel away the backing and arrange the shapes on the bag fabric. Iron the shapes to fuse them in place, then secure them with machine stitching.

4 Fold the towel in half with right sides facing so the short edges meet; pin and stitch the side seams and turn the bag right sides out.

5 For the drawstring loops, fold the towelling rectangles in half so the long edges meet. Pin and stitch the long edges together. Turn right sides out then press a 1cm (¹/₂in) turning at each end. Pin and stitch the loops evenly around the bag, 5cm (2in) from the top edge, then thread the cord through the loops and knot the ends.

Beach towel

1 Use the photocopied templates to trace two small fish, two large starfish (stars) and two small starfish onto fusible bonding. Iron fusible bonding onto towelling scraps, cut out the shapes, peel away the backing and arrange the shapes on one end of the towel. (Towelling scraps will be able to cope with constant washing during the summer months.) Iron the shapes in place, then secure them with machine zigzag stitching.

2 Draw the fish eyes with a fabric marker pen, then iron to fix them. Finally, stitch the decorative braid along the edge in a wavy line.

Goldie and Fluff

Goldie and Fluff are a pair of cheeky rag dolls made of calico, felt and cotton scraps. Both dolls are based on the same pattern, with calico faces and arms, cotton check bodies and stripy legs and they are 42cm (16½in) tall. The patterned bodies and legs look like clothing, so all you have to do is add the skirt or shorts to complete their outfits. Both characters have squashy calico noses, buttons for eyes and recycled wool (yarn) for hair.

WHAT YOU NEED:

Photocopy of rag-doll patterns (see pages 112-113)
Scissors
Calico for head and arms
Check fabric for body and sleeves
Striped fabric for legs
Fabric for patches and skirt or trousers
Felt for shoes • Sewing needle
Sewing thread and pins
Wadding (batting) or other filling
Stranded embroidery cotton (floss)
Embroidery needle • Buttons
Fine wool (yarn) for hair
Large-eyed needle

Rag dolls

Note: You'll find full-size patterns for the dolls on pages 112-113 to make a doll 42cm (16½in high). Seam allowances of 6mm (¼in) have been added to all the pattern pieces. Transfer all marks and notches from the pattern pieces to the fabric pieces.

Cutting list for each doll:
In calico: four lower arms, two heads and one nose.
In check fabric: four sleeves and two bodies.
In striped fabric: two legs.
In felt: four shoes.
In contrasting fabric: two or more small squares for patches.
For Goldie: 18 x 52cm (7 x 20½in) rectangle of check fabric for her skirt; two 6 x 65cm (2¼ x 25½in) matching strips for the frills.
For Fluff: four shorts in contrast fabric and four matching braces.

1 With right sides facing, pin each calico head to a body. Stitch in place between the dots. Press the seams towards the head.
2 To make the arms, pin each lower arm to a sleeve with right sides facing so the short straight edges and notches match. Stitch in place then press the seams. With right sides facing, pin two arms together, then tack (baste) and stitch around the edges, leaving the top edge open. Turn the arm right sides out. Fill the hand with wadding (batting) then machine stitch across the top of the hand to keep the wadding (batting) in place. Lightly stuff the rest of the arm to within 3.5cm (1½in) of the top edge, then work rows of running stitches

(see page 11) around the top of each arm so you can gather up the arms to fit the shoulders.

3 To make the legs, place two shoes together with right sides facing. Pin and stitch the front curved edges together, then press the seams open, snipping into the seam allowance for ease where necessary. Pin the stitched shoe to a leg with right sides facing, so that the stitched shoe seam matches the notch on the bottom edge of the leg (fig. 26). Stitch the seam then repeat to make and attach the other shoe to the other leg. Press the seams towards the leg.

4 With right sides facing, fold each leg in half, then pin, tack (baste) and stitch along the leg and shoe edges, leaving the top edge open. Turn the leg right sides out, then lightly fill with polyester wadding (batting) to within 3.5cm (1½in) of the top edge.

5 To assemble the doll's body, lay out one joined body and head, right side up. Pull up the threads of running stitches along the top of each arm to gather the edge so it fits between the dots on the body shape. Pin the arms and legs over the body front so they face inwards, and so all the raw edges and notches match (fig. 27). Make sure that both feet face in or out. Pin and stitch the arms and legs close to the raw edges to secure them.

6 Place the remaining head and body shape on top, right side down, so the arms and legs are sandwiched between the two layers. Pin, tack (baste) and stitch around the edges, leaving a gap at the bottom for stuffing. Clip the seam allowances where necessary for ease. Carefully turn the doll right sides out, so the arms and legs are now on the outside. Fill the head and body with polyester wadding (batting), then close the opening by oversewing or with slipstitches.

7 To make the doll's nose, work rows of running stitches around the edge of the calico nose. Place some wadding (batting) at the centre of the shape, pull up the threads to gather the edges and enclose the wadding (batting), then secure the gathering threads with a knot. Stitch the nose to the doll's face with small stitches, then stitch two buttons above the nose for the eyes.

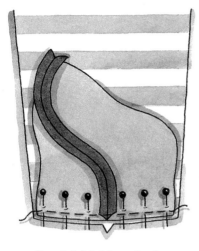

fig. 26 Making the legs

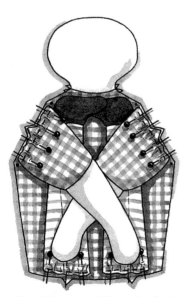

fig. 27 Assembling the body

Goldie

1 With right sides facing, fold the skirt in half so the short edges meet. Pin and stitch the short edges together, then press the seam open. Use embroidery cotton (floss) to attach the small patches to the skirt with running stitches, then tease out the threads around the edges of each patch to fray them.

2 To make the skirt frill, pin the two fabric strips together with right sides facing and stitch the short edges together; press the seams open. Stitch a small hem along one long edge and work two rows of

running stitches for gathering along the other long edge.

3 With right sides facing, pin the skirt frill and bottom skirt edges together so that the raw edges match. Pull up the gathering threads to make the frill fit around the skirt, then distribute the gathers evenly. Tack (baste) and stitch in place.

4 Work two rows of running stitches for gathering around the top edge of the skirt. With right sides facing, place the skirt upside down over the doll, so that the skirt and frill cover the doll's head and the raw edge is roughly at her waist. Pull up the gathering threads to make the skirt fit around the body, then distribute the gathers evenly. Pin, tack (baste) and hand stitch the skirt to the doll's body (see fig. 28), then turn the skirt down to cover the doll's legs. To finish the dress, stitch buttons down the front and a row of running stitch in embroidery cotton (floss) along the frill edge.

5 For Goldie's hair, scrunch up a bundle of curly unpicked wool (yarn), then stitch it down at intervals along the curved seam on the doll's head. Finish by stitching a small bow at the front – you can make one or buy one ready-made.

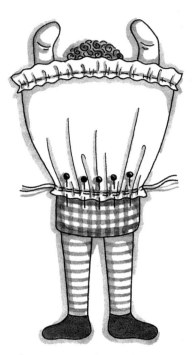

fig. 28 Attaching the skirt

Fluff

1 With right sides facing, pin two shorts together. Tack (baste) and then stitch the straight side seams together then press the seams open. Repeat for the remaining shorts shapes. Turn one leg right sides out and place it inside the other leg so that the right sides are facing and the curved edges match (fig. 29). Pin, tack (baste) and stitch along the curved edge, then turn the shorts right sides out.

2 Stitch small patches on each leg with running stitches using embroidery cotton (floss), then fray the edges of each patch. Turn a 1.5cm (⁵⁄₈in) hem at the waist and legs, then stitch in place with running stitches using embroidery cotton (floss).

3 To make the braces, pin two cotton braces together with right sides facing, so that the short diagonal edges match. Stitch the short diagonal edges, then press the seams open. Press a 6mm (¹⁄₄in) hem along the long edges of each braces shape, then stitch in place with running stitches using embroidery cotton (floss).

4 Lay the braces over the doll's body, so the shoulder seams match. Secure them at the shoulder with hand stitches. Put the shorts on the doll, stitch the shorts waist to the braces at the front and back, then stitch small buttons onto the waist where the braces join.

5 For Fluff's hair, thread a double length of tapestry wool (yarn) into a large-eyed needle. Thread short lengths at intervals along the curved seam on the head. Secure each length by tying a double knot so the ends of the wool (yarn) stick out in different directions.

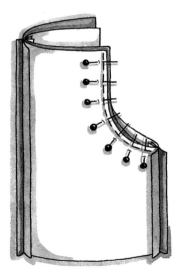

fig. 29 Making the shorts

Sad old bear

'My sad old bear has got no fur. He's got buttons for eyes and patches to keep his stuffing in, but I love him.' This sentimental verse sums up the feelings that children and adults everywhere have for their teddy bears. The picture and pyjama case in this chapter highlight that verse and feature a well-loved bear which has lost none of its cuddly appeal despite all his patches.

Bear picture

♥

WHAT YOU NEED:

Picture frame • Scissors
Base fabric, such as
check cotton
Fusible bonding • Calico
Hessian (jute) • Pencil
Iron
Felt and fabric scraps
Sewing thread
Dressmaker's chalk pencil
Fabric marker pen
Stranded embroidery
cotton (floss)
Embroidery needle
Buttons

1 Carefully remove the backing board from the picture frame and use this as a template to cut a rectangle of fabric for the picture base and a rectangle of fusible bonding the same size. Cut a rectangle of calico slightly smaller than the base fabric, and a hessian (jute) rectangle smaller still, but larger than the bear template (page 123).

2 Trace around the bear outline on page 123, then trace the shapes for the ears, nose and patches and five small hearts from page 117 separately onto fusible bonding. Iron the bonding onto small fabric and felt scraps. Cut out all the shapes, peel away the backing and arrange them on the hessian (jute) rectangle.

3 Lay the hessian (jute) rectangle right side up over the centre of the calico shape and join by machine stitching 1cm (1/2in) inside each edge. Lay the joined fabrics right side up over the centre of the backing fabric and machine stitch 1.5cm (5/8in) inside each edge. Finish the outer edges of the calico and hessian (jute) by teasing out the threads to fray them.

4 Use the chalk pencil to write the verse around the calico border and to mark the mouth and seams on the bear. Draw over the chalk marks with a fabric marker pen, then press the fabric from the wrong side to fix it. Cut out and fuse the border hearts and patches in place, then use embroidery cotton (floss) to work straight stitches around each patch. Define the border on the calico in running stitch with embroidery cotton (floss). Stitch on the buttons.

5 To finish the picture, iron bonding onto the wrong side of the base fabric, peel away the backing and lay the fabric over the backing board. Iron in place, then frame the picture.

Bear pyjama case

WHAT YOU NEED:

Scissors • Calico

Tape measure

Dressmaker's chalk pencil

Fabric marker pen

Photocopy of bear template

(see page 123)

Fusible bonding • Iron

Felt and fabric scraps

Stranded embroidery

cotton (floss)

Embroidery needle

Buttons

Sewing needle and pins

Sewing thread

1 For the pyjama case front, cut a 34 x 46cm (13½ x 18in) rectangle of calico. For the case back, cut two calico rectangles, each two-thirds the size of the case front (see page 16).

2 Using fig. 30, below, as your reference, draw a 5cm (2in) wide border on the calico front and write the verse with a chalk pencil. Draw over the verse with a fabric marker pen, then press the fabric from the wrong side to fix it.

3 Trace around the bear outline on your photocopy, then trace the arms, nose, ears and patches separately onto fusible bonding; draw the patch and five small hearts from page 117 for the border onto fusible bonding, too. Iron the bonding onto the wrong side of felt and fabric scraps. Cut out the shapes, peel away the backing and arrange them on the calico front, then iron the shapes in place.

4 Use embroidery cotton (floss) to work running stitches around the bear's body and to indicate the seams on his tummy, neck, arms and legs. Work the mouth in backstitch and add straight stitches around each patch for decoration. Stitch on the buttons for eyes, then outline the border in cross stitch. (See page 10-11 for details on working all these embroidery stitches).

5 For the case back, hem one long edge of each calico rectangle. Lay the appliquéd calico front on a flat surface, right side up and pin the calico backs on top, right sides down, so all the raw edges match and the hemmed edges overlap at the centre.

6 Tack (baste) the layers together, then stitch around all four edges, taking a 1.5cm (⅝in) seam allowance. Trim the seam allowances at the corners for ease, turn the case right sides out and press it lightly.

fig. 30 Bear design

My sad old bear

has got no fur. He's got for

him.

his stuffing in, but I

eyes and to keep

Halloween

*I*t's Halloween, when children everywhere drape themselves in sinister garments, cover their faces in bloodcurdling make-up and stalk the streets after dark, terrifying adults at every turn. Join in the fun by making this collection of spooky things out of hessian (jute), felt and fabric scraps. The ghastly ghosts and cheeky pumpkins make excellent designs for cards, and they are joined by gruesome bats on a trick-or-treat bag and a wonderful Halloween wreath that is made even more sinister by the small bundles of twigs, used by witches to make their broomsticks.

Spooky cards

♥

WHAT YOU NEED:

Card rectangles (A4 size is ideal) • Scissors Hessian (jute) or fabric Photocopy of Halloween templates (see page 117) Fusible bonding Iron • Felt scraps Stranded embroidery cotton (floss) Embroidery needle Fabric marker pen Sewing thread

1 Fold each card in half so the short edges meet. Cut a piece of hessian (jute) or fabric slightly smaller than the folded card.
2 Trace the shapes of your chosen motif(s) – pumpkins or spooky ghost – from your photocopy onto fusible bonding. Iron the fusible bonding onto felt scraps and cut out the shapes. Peel away the backing and arrange the felt shapes on the hessian (jute) or fabric. Iron them to fuse them in place, then add a decorative outline of running stitch (see page 11) around each one with embroidery cotton (floss). Mark the eyes with a fabric marker pen in a colour which shows up well on the fabric.
3 Centre the appliquéd fabric right side up over the folded card and machine stitch 1cm (1/2in) from each edge of the fabric. Finish the outer edges of the fabric by teasing out the threads to fray them. To do this, use a needle or your fingers to prise out the cross threads along each edge to a depth of about 3-6mm (1/8-1/4in). Snip the vertical threads at intervals, if necessary.

Trick-or-treat bag

♥

WHAT YOU NEED:

Scissors • Tape measure

Hessian (jute)

Check fabric

Photocopies or tracings of

Halloween templates in

various sizes (see page 117)

Fusible bonding • Iron

Felt and calico scraps

Sewing thread and pins

Stranded embroidery cotton

(floss) and embroidery

needle (optional)

Fabric marker pen • Glue

1 From hessian (jute) cut a 34 x 76cm (13½ x 30in) rectangle. From check fabric cut two 8 x 34cm (3¼ x 13½in) strips for the edging and two 9 x 36cm (3½ x 14¼in) handle strips. Fold the hessian in half so the short edges meet.

2 Trace two bats, a ghost and two pumpkins from your photocopies or tracings onto fusible bonding. Iron the bonding onto felt, cut out the shapes, peel away the backing and arrange the shapes on the hessian (jute) bag front. Iron the shapes in place, then unfold the hessian (jute) and secure the shapes with machine stitching. Work small cross stitches (see page 10) in embroidery cotton (floss) for the eyes or use a fabric marker pen, then glue on the felt noses.

3 Cut a small calico patch and write 'TRICK OR TREAT' on it with a fabric marker pen. Iron the patch on the wrong side to fix the letters. Cut another slightly larger patch from check fabric. Stitch the check patch onto the hessian (jute) bag front and machine stitch 1cm (½in) from each edge. Lay the calico patch right side up, over the check patch and machine stitch 1cm (½in) from each edge,

then tease out the threads on both patches to fray the edges.

4 Use the check fabric edging strips to bind the short edges of the bag (see page 17). Fold the appliquéd hessian (jute) in half with right sides facing. Pin and then stitch the side seams, taking a 1.5cm (5/8in) seam allowance, then turn the bag right sides out. To make the handles, press a 1.5cm (5/8in) turning along each long edge of each handle strip, then press each strip in half and stitch along the length. Stitch the ends to the top edge of the bag.

Halloween wreath

WHAT YOU NEED:

Scissors
Polyester wadding (batting)
Hessian (jute)
Sewing thread and needle
Photocopies or tracings of Halloween templates (see page 117)
Felt scraps • Pins
Stranded embroidery cotton (floss)
Embroidery needle
Multi-purpose glue
Small twigs
String or cord

1 Cut a 50 x 90cm (20 x 36in) strip of polyester wadding (batting), and enough 8cm (3in) wide hessian (jute) strips to cut and join into a 7m (7⅝yd) length. Join the strips, then tease out the threads on both sides to fray the edges. Keep the pulled threads to use later.

2 Tightly roll the strip of polyester wadding (batting) into a long, narrow sausage shape, stitch along the length to secure the loose edge, then bend it into a ring and stitch both ends together. Gently wind the long hessian (jute) strip around the ring to cover the wadding (batting), and stitch the end in place.

3 Cut out the photocopied or traced bat, ghost and pumpkin templates and use them as patterns to cut shapes from felt. For each bat and ghost cut two pattern pieces; for each pumpkin cut two pumpkin shapes and one stalk.

4 To make the padded shapes, pin the pairs of felt pieces together. Work running stitches around the edges of each shape with embroidery cotton (floss), leaving a gap to fill them. Fill with wadding (batting), then complete the stitching. Use stranded cotton (floss) to work small cross stitches (see page 10) for the eyes and the bat's mouth, then glue on the felt noses. Stitch the pumpkin stalks on the padded pumpkins.

5 Arrange the padded shapes around the wreath and glue in place. Scrunch up bundles of the hessian (jute) threads you removed in step 1 and glue them in the gaps between the padded shapes, then tie up small bundles of twigs with string or cord and glue them on top of the scrunched threads. Stitch a small hanging loop of string or cord to the back of the wreath.

Autumn leaves

This collection of winter warmers and accessories was inspired by the magical colours and shapes of autumn leaves. Oak, maple, hawthorn and cotoneaster leaves with acorns and berries adorn a stunning throw, a handsome draught excluder, a wall hanging and practical hessian (jute) gardener's apron. A fabulous wreath made from old Indian-cotton skirts in autumn shades of greens and browns completes the collection. Copy the colours and motifs here or use the idea to make your own collection for spring, summer or even winter.

Appliquéd leaf throw

WHAT YOU NEED:

*Pre-washed and dyed
woollen blanket
Tape measure • Scissors
Sewing thread
Photocopies of autumn leaf
templates in various sizes
(see page 125)
Fusible bonding • Iron
Fabric and felt scraps
Sewing thread
Tapestry wool (yarn)
Embroidery needle*

1 Cut a square of pre-washed and dyed woollen blanket to the size you want your finished throw, adding 1cm (1/2in) seam allowances all the way round. Pin and then machine stitch a 1cm (1/2in) hem all the way round.

2 Because the throw is so large, it's easier to work out your design before you cut the appliqué shapes from fabric. Cut out the photocopied shapes and arrange them around the border and at the centre of the throw.

3 Work out how many of each shape you will need, then trace the shapes onto fusible bonding. Iron the bonding onto the wrong side of felt and fabric scraps, cut out the shapes, peel away the backing and arrange the shapes on the throw fabric. Iron the shapes to fuse them in place, then secure them with machine stitching.

4 To finish the throw, use tapestry wool (yarn) in a toning colour to work blanket stitch over the turned edges of the throw and a border of cross stitch at the centre. (See pages 10-11 for details on working embroidery stitches.)

Gardener's apron

WHAT YOU NEED:

*Tape measure • Scissors
Hessian (jute)
Cotton webbing
Needle and sewing thread
Photocopy of leaf and berry
templates (see page 125)
Fusible bonding
Iron • Felt scraps*

1 From hessian (jute) cut one 48 x 65cm (19 x 25 1/2in) rectangle for the apron and one 28 x 65cm (11 x 25 1/2in) rectangle for the pocket, then cut two 60cm (23 1/2in) lengths of cotton webbing for the apron ties.

2 Find the centre line of the pocket by folding the small hessian (jute) rectangle in half so the short edges meet. Mark the fold (centre) with tacking (basting) stitches.

3 Trace the photocopied leaf shapes onto fusible bonding. Iron the fusible bonding onto felt scraps, cut out the shapes, peel away the backing and arrange the shapes either side of the tacked (basted) line on the pocket. Iron the shapes in place, then secure them by machine stitching close to the edge of each one. Stitch a 2.5cm (1in) hem along the top edge of the pocket.

4 Lay the pocket over the apron with right sides up and the side and bottom edges matching. Pin and tack (baste) the layers together. Machine stitch along the tacked (basted) pocket centre line to make two pockets. Press 1.5cm (5/8in), then 4cm (1 3/4in) to the right side along the top of the apron and stitch in place. Stitch a 1.5cm (5/8in) turning to the wrong side around the remaining side and bottom edges of the apron. Stitch the ties to the apron sides.

Draught excluder

♥

WHAT YOU NEED:

Scissors • Tape measure

Pre-washed and dyed

woollen blanket

Paper and pencil • Card

Polyester wadding (batting)

Felt and fabric scraps

Photocopy of leaf and berry

templates (see page 125)

Fusible bonding • Iron

Sewing thread

Pins and needle

Pair of old tights

Rice or kitty litter

1 Cut a 42 x 80cm (16^1/$_2$ x 31^1/$_2$in) rectangle of woollen blanket. Draw a 6cm (2^1/$_4$in) diameter circle on paper to make a pattern and use it to cut two card and two wadding (batting) circles. Cut two more circles of contrasting fabric, this time adding 1.5cm (^{5}/$_8$in) all the way round.

2 Find the centre line by folding the woollen fabric rectangle in half so that the long edges meet. Mark the fold (centre) with tacking (basting) stitches.

3 Trace the photocopied leaf and berry shapes onto fusible bonding. Iron the fusible bonding onto the wrong side of felt and fabric scraps, cut out the shapes, peel away the backing and arrange the shapes along the tacked (basted) line. Iron the shapes to fuse them in place, then secure them by machine stitching close to the edge of each one. Remove the tacking (basting) stitches.

4 With right sides facing, bring the long edges of the woollen fabric together. Pin and stitch the seam, then turn right sides out. Fill one leg of the tights with rice or kitty litter and tie a knot at the end.

Put this inside the tube, fill the rest of the tube with polyester wadding (batting), then work a line of running stitches at each end of the tube and pull up the threads to gather the fabric and close the gaps at each end.

5 Work a row of running stitches around each fabric circle for gathering, then lay the circles right sides down. Place the wadding (batting), then card circles centrally over each fabric circle, then pull up and secure the threads so that the edges of the fabric gather up and over the padded card. Stitch a padded circle to each end of the draught excluder to cover any raw edges.

Wall hanging

1 Cut a square of pre-washed woollen blanket and a square of wadding (batting) the size you want your wall hanging to be. Cut a square of backing fabric 2.5cm (1in) larger all the way round.
2 Lay the blanket square over the wadding (batting), then pin and tack (baste) the two layers together (see pages 14-15). Mark a grid of nine squares with tacking (basting) stitches on the padded fabric, then quilt along the tacked lines with three rows of running stitches (see page 11) using embroidery cotton (floss).
3 Because the fabric is so large, it's a good idea to work out your design before you cut out the shapes. To do this trace the photocopied shapes onto paper (or make more photocopies), cut them out and arrange them in the grid sections on the quilted fabric.
4 Work out how many of each shape you will need, then trace the shapes onto fusible bonding. Iron the bonding onto felt scraps, cut out the shapes, peel away the backing and arrange the shapes on the quilted fabric. Iron the shapes in place. Use embroidery cotton (floss) to secure the edges of each shape with running stitches, then stitch a small cross stitch (see page 10) on some berries and at the end of each acorn.
5 Centre the padded appliqué blanket square right side up over the backing fabric, then pin and tack (baste) the two layers together. To bind the edges, press a 1cm (¹/₂in) turning all round the backing fabric, then fold the turning over the edges of the appliquéd square. Pin and stitch in place. Cut four strips of cotton webbing the same length and fold them in half to make hanging loops. Stitch them to the top of the hanging at regular intervals, then thread a stick through the loops to hang the banner.

Rag wreath

WHAT YOU NEED:

Scissors or pinking shears
Fabric scraps
Half-rounded polystyrene ring
Blunt pencil

1 Use pinking shears or scissors to cut 5cm (2in) squares from cotton fabric scraps. (Pinking shears are best because they give a nicely finished edge to the squares.) For a 26cm (10¼in) ring you will need about 450-500 fabric squares.

2 Place the blunt pencil at the centre of each square and use it to poke the square into the polystyrene ring. Cover the front of the ring completely, leaving the flat back bare so you can hang it against a wall.

Kids' bedroom

Most children adore the bright colours and simple shapes of the appliqué designs in this book. So here, many of the motifs from other chapters have been used to create a bright collection of accessories for a kids' room. You can use whichever motifs your children like the most. To make this collection really lively, scraps of fabrics and old woollen blankets were gathered together and dyed strong purple and bright orange to create the main colours for the projects. Dyed calico, gingham, cotton fabrics and a recycled tablecloth complete the colourful effect.

Appliquéd bedspread

1 Cut a 1.3 x 1.6m (1³/₈ x 1³/₄yd) rectangle of pre-washed and dyed woollen blanket for the bedspread; cut twelve 26cm (10¹/₄in) squares from blanket or felt. Machine stitch a 1cm (¹/₂in) turning all the way round the bedspread, then use contrasting tapestry wool (yarn) to work blanket stitch (see page 10) over the turned edges.

2 Cut out the photocopied templates and use them as patterns to trace an assortment of twelve hearts and stars onto fusible bonding. Iron the bonding onto fabric scraps, cut out the shapes, peel away the backing and place one shape in the centre of each blanket square. Iron the hearts and stars to fuse them in place, then secure them with machine stitching.

3 Arrange the appliquéd squares in rows on the bedspread. Pin, tack (baste) and machine stitch them in place, then use tapestry wool (yarn) in contrasting colours to work decorative running stitches around each appliquéd shape. Finally, work a border of big, bold cross stitch (see page 10) around each square and around the edge of the bedspread.

Appliquéd rug

1 Cut two 63 x 93cm (24³/₄ x 36¹/₂in) rectangles of blanket – one for the front and one for the back. To work out your design, trace the photocopied shapes onto paper, cut them out and arrange them on the rug front.

2 Work out how many of each shape you will need, then trace those shapes onto fusible bonding. Iron the bonding onto blanket or felt scraps, cut out the shapes, peel away the backing and arrange the shapes on the rug front. Iron the shapes in place, then secure them with machine stitching.

3 With right sides facing, pin the rug front and back together, so all the raw outer edges match. Pin and tack (baste) the layers in place, then stitch around all four edges, taking a 1.5cm (⁵/₈in) seam allowance and leaving a gap for turning. Trim the seam allowances at the corners, turn the rug out and close the gap by oversewing.

4 To finish the rug, use tapestry wool (yarn) to work blanket stitch around the edges and then to work a border of cross stitch. Work running stitch around some of the appliquéd shapes, stitching through all the fabric layers, for decoration and to keep the layers together. (See pages 10-11 for details on embroidery stitches.)

Height chart

♥

WHAT YOU NEED:

Plastic coat hanger
Paper and pencil
Scissors
Backing fabric
Base fabric, such a
dyed gingham
Calico
Fabric marker pen • Iron
Sewing thread and pins
Long ruler
Photocopies of boat, sun,
cloud and small fish
templates in the sizes you
require (see pages 122-123)
Fusible bonding
Felt and fabric scraps
Polyester wadding (batting)
Piping cord • Buttons

1 Lay the coat hanger on a piece of paper and draw around it (see page 32, step 1); mark the position of the hook. Add 2cm (3/4in) for ease plus 1.5cm (5/8in) seam allowances around the curved edges and 4cm (13/4in) at the bottom straight edge, then use this as a pattern to cut two shapes of backing fabric. Cut one long rectangle of both backing fabric and base fabric, 112cm (44in) long by the width of the straight edge of the coat-hanger shape.

2 Cut a small calico patch and write 'I am This Big!' on it with a fabric marker pen; iron on the wrong side to fix the words. Pin and machine stitch the patch to the right side of one coat-hanger shape, then fray the edges by teasing out the threads.

3 Pin the coat-hanger shapes together with right sides facing. Tack (baste) the layers together, then stitch around the curved edges, leaving a gap at the very top for the coat-hanger hook. Turn right sides out, insert the coat hanger, then press a 1cm (1/2in) hem along the straight lower edges and stitch together.

4 Cut an 8 x 104cm (31/4 x 41in) strip of calico. Use a fabric maker pen to copy the lines and measurements from the ruler onto the calico. Press the fabric from the wrong side to fix the marks, then stitch the strip down the right-hand side of the base fabric rectangle. Tease out the threads from the edges of the calico to fray them.

5 Cut out the photocopies and arrange them on the base rectangle to calculate how many you require of each shape. Trace the shapes you want onto fusible bonding, iron the bonding onto the wrong side of contrasting fabric scraps and cut out. Peel away the backing and arrange the shapes on the base fabric to the left of the calico strip. Iron them in place, then secure the shapes with machine stitching.

6 For the padded fish height indicator, cut out two felt fish. Pin the fish together and stitch around the edges, leaving a gap for filling. Stuff the fish with wadding (batting), then stitch the gap closed. Draw an eye with a fabric marker pen. Cut a small felt strip, pin it to the back of the fish, along the length, then stitch the ends in place to form a loop to hang it from the cord.

7 Trim the cord so it's the same length as the calico ruler and tie a knot at one end, thread on the fish, then tie a knot in the other end. Stitch the knotted ends next to the calico strip.

8 With right sides facing, pin the appliquéd rectangle and backing fabric together. Machine stitch around the edges, leaving a gap at the top for turning. Trim the seam allowances at the corners for ease, then turn the chart right sides out. Stitch the top of the chart to the base of the coat-hanger cover, then stitch buttons along the join.

Toy bags

WHAT YOU NEED:

Scissors • Tape measure
Base fabric, such as
dyed gingham
Calico
Contrasting fabric
Photocopy of chosen
template (see pages
115-126)
Fusible bonding • Iron
Felt or fabric scrap
for the motif
Sewing thread and pins

1 Cut a 48 x 118cm (19 x 46^1/$_2$in) rectangle of base fabric. With wrong sides facing, fold the fabric in half, so that both short edges meet. The fold is the bottom of the bag. Cut a 20 x 22cm (7^3/$_4$ x 8^3/$_4$in) patch of calico. For the drawstring channels, cut two 7 x 45cm (2^3/$_4$ x 17^3/$_4$in) strips of contrasting fabric; cut two 7 x 70cm (2^3/$_4$ x 27^1/$_2$in) strips of contrasting fabric for the drawstrings.

2 Trace the photocopied template onto fusible bonding. Iron the fusible bonding onto the wrong side of a felt or fabric scrap, cut out the shape, peel away the backing and centre it on the calico patch. Iron the shape in place and secure it by machine stitching close to the edge. Pin and stitch the patch on the bag front 1.5cm (5/8in) from the calico edges, then tease out the threads on the calico to fray the edges.

3 Press a 1cm (1/2in) turning all the way round each channel strip. With right sides facing up, centre a channel strip over the unfolded base fabric, 7cm (2^3/$_4$in) from each short edge. Tack (baste) the strips in place, then stitch along each long edge of each strip, leaving the short edges open to form the drawstring channels.

4 Fold the bag fabric in half with right sides facing so the short edges meet. Pin and stitch the two long side seams, taking a 1.5cm (5/8in) seam allowance. Trim the seam allowances at the corners. Stitch a 1.5cm (5/8in) hem along the top edge, then turn the bag right sides out.

5 Press a 1cm (1/2in) turning along each long edge of each drawstring strip, then press each strip in half so the folded edges meet and stitch along the length. Thread each drawstring through both channels and knot the ends together.

Toy tidy

WHAT YOU NEED:

Tape measure • Scissors
Base fabric, such as
dyed blanket
Backing fabric, such as
dyed blanket
Bright fabrics
Sewing thread
Photocopies of your
favourite templates (see
pages 115-126)
Fusible bonding • Iron
Felt and fabric scraps
Decorative braid (optional)
Sewing needle and pins
Stranded embroidery cotton
Embroidery needle
Stick for hanging

1 Cut one 67 x 79cm (26½ x 31in) rectangle of base fabric and one of backing fabric. From bright fabrics cut four 20 x 28cm (8 x 11in) rectangles and one 20 x 45cm (8 x 17¾in) rectangle for the pockets; cut seven 9 x 14cm (3½ x 5½in) strips for the hanging loops.

2 To make the pockets, stitch a 1.5cm (⅝in) turning along the top edge, then press a 1.5cm (⅝in) turning along the remaining edges. Trace your chosen template shapes onto fusible bonding. Iron the bonding onto the wrong side of felt and fabric scraps, cut out the shapes, peel away the backing and arrange the fabric shapes on each pocket. Iron the shapes in place and secure with machine stitches. Add decorative braid around some shapes, if required. Using embroidery cotton, work rows of cross stitches (see page 10) across the top of each pocket shape.

3 Arrange the pockets in two vertical columns on the base fabric, with three smaller pockets in one column, and a small and large pocket in the other column. Leave a border of 7.5cm (3in) along the top edge, and 5cm (2in) around the side and bottom edges. Pin, tack (baste) and stitch the pockets in place.

4 For the hanging loops, fold the strips in half, so the right sides are facing and the long edges meet. Pin, tack (baste) and stitch along the long edge of each one, taking a 1cm (⅜in) seam allowance, then turn right sides out. Centre the seam on one side and press. Fold each strip in half so the short edges meet and the seam is on the inside, then pin along the top edge of the base fabric so the right sides are facing and the raw edges match. With right sides facing, pin, tack (baste) and stitch the appliquéd front to the backing fabric, taking a 1.5cm (⅝in) seam allowance and leaving a gap for turning (see fig. 23, page 45). Trim the seam allowances diagonally at the corners, then turn the toy tidy right sides out. Topstitch around the edge. Press the tidy and thread a stick through the loops to hang it by.

Autumn rabbit cushions

These stylish autumn cushions use a template based on an old mediaeval terracotta tile design, showing a rabbit sitting in the undergrowth surrounded by trees and acorns. Calico, felt and embroidery thread are all you need to make these simple but effective designs using appliqué and quilting techniques. The designs have been kept very simple, but you could add a decorative border, braid or fringing around the cushion edges to make them really sumptuous.

♥

WHAT YOU NEED:

Scissors • Tape measure
Square cushion pad
Calico
Photocopy of rabbit template
(see page 124)
Fusible bonding
Iron • Felt
Stranded embroidery
cotton (floss)
Embroidery needle
Sewing needle and pins
Sewing thread

Appliquéd cushion

1 Cut a square of calico the size of your cushion pad, adding 1.5cm (⅝in) seam allowances all the way round. For the cushion back, cut two pieces of calico, each two-thirds the size of the cushion front (see page 16).

2 To create your appliquéd design, use your photocopied rabbit template as a pattern to trace all the shapes onto fusible bonding and iron the bonding onto felt. Cut out the shapes, peel away the backing and arrange them centrally on the calico cushion front. Iron the shapes in place, then hand stitch around each one using running stitch with contrasting embroidery cotton (floss). Press the design on the wrong side.

3 For the cushion back, hem one long edge of each calico rectangle. Lay the appliquéd calico shape on a flat surface, right side up. With right sides down, place the calico backs over the appliquéd calico, so that all the raw outer edges match and the hemmed edges overlap at the centre.

4 Pin and tack (baste) the layers in place, then stitch around all four edges taking a 1.5cm (⅝in) seam allowance. Trim the seam allowances at the corners. Turn the cover through to the right side and insert the square cushion pad.

Quilted cushion

♥

WHAT YOU NEED:

Scissors • Tape measure
Square cushion pad
Calico
Polyester wadding (batting)
Photocopy of rabbit template
(see page 124)
Dressmaker's carbon paper
Sewing thread and needle
Quilting or slate frame
(optional)
Stranded embroidery
cotton (floss)
Embroidery needle • Iron

1 Cut two squares of calico the size of your cushion pad and one of wadding (batting), adding 1.5cm (⅝in) seam allowances all the way round each one. For the cushion back, cut two pieces of calico, each two-thirds the size of the cushion front (see page 16).

2 Transfer the photocopied template design to the right side of one calico square using dressmaker's carbon in a colour close to the fabric colour (see page 9).

3 Sandwich the calico and padding together so the padding is in the middle and the top layer of calico has the transferred design facing out. Pin and tack (baste) all three layers together (see pages 14-15). If you have one, mount the work in a quilting or slate frame. Work around the lines of the design using small running stitches or backstitch (see pages 10-11) with contrasting embroidery cotton. Press the quilted design from the wrong side.

4 For the cushion back, hem one long edge of each calico rectangle. Lay the quilted calico square on a flat surface, right side up. With right sides down, place the calico backs over the quilted calico square, so that all the raw edges match and the hemmed edges overlap at the centre.

5 Pin and tack (baste) the layers in place, then stitch around all four edges, taking a 1.5cm (⅝in) seam allowance. Trim the seam allowances at the corners. Turn the cover right sides out and insert the cushion pad.

Paisley bedroom

A beautiful paisley shawl from the early 1800s inspired this pretty design for a lady's bedroom. The appliquéd paisley motif is edged with lace and then embroidered with simple flowers. For an authentic look, choose a dark colour for the appliqué shape and stranded cottons in fresh colours for the embroidery. The hot-water bottle cover, nightdress case and cushion are made from an old woollen blanket, dyed to a soft shade of blue.

Paisley cushion

WHAT YOU NEED:

Scissors • Tape measure
Pre-washed and dyed
woollen blanket
Square cushion pad
Fusible bonding
Iron • Felt
Sewing thread and pins
Dressmaker's chalk pencil
Pre-gathered lace edging
Stranded embroidery
cotton (floss)
Embroidery needle
Tapestry wool (yarn)

1 Cut a square of blanket to the size of your cushion pad, adding 1cm (¹/₂in) seam allowances all the way round. For the cushion back, cut two rectangles of blanket, each two-thirds the size of the cushion front (see page 16).

2 Trace the paisley template (see page 124) onto fusible bonding and iron the bonding onto felt. Cut out the shape, peel away the backing and centre the shape on the blanket front. Iron the shape in place, then secure with machine stitches. Use a chalk pencil to draw round the shape with a curl spiralling from the top, then pin and machine stitch the lace edging along this line.

3 Use the chalk pencil to mark the positions of flowers and petals on and around the appliquéd motif. Work the petals and leaves on the motif in lazy-daisy stitch, using embroidery cotton (floss). Work the flower centres with small cross stitches. (See pages 10-11 for details on working embroidery stitches.) Now use tapestry wool (yarn) to work the flowers and leaves which surround the motif, using the same embroidery stitches.

4 For the cushion backs, hem one long edge of each blanket rectangle with blanket stitches in tapestry wool (yarn). Lay the cushion front right side down, then place the blanket backs right sides up on top, so that all the raw outer edges match and the hemmed edges overlap at the centre. Pin and tack (baste) the layers together, then use tapestry wool (yarn) to work blanket stitch around all four edges; insert the cushion pad.

Hot-water bottle cover

♥

WHAT YOU NEED:

Hot-water bottle

Scissors

Pre-washed and dyed

woollen blanket

Tape measure

Fusible bonding

Iron • Felt

Dressmaker's chalk pencil

Pre-gathered lace edging

Sewing thread and pins

Stranded embroidery

cotton (floss)

Embroidery needle

Tapestry wool (yarn)

1 To make a paper pattern, draw round a hot-water bottle, adding 2.5cm (1in) seam allowances all the way round, then cut one shape from blanket for the cover back. For the front, cut two pieces of blanket, each just over half the size of the cover back, so that the two front pieces overlap by 7.5cm (3in).

2 Trace two paisley motifs (see page 124) onto fusible bonding and iron the bonding onto felt. Cut out the shapes, peel away the backing and arrange one shape on each front piece. Iron the shapes in place, then secure with machine stitches. Use a chalk pencil to draw round the shapes with a curl spiralling from the top, then pin and machine stitch the lace edging along this line.

3 Mark the positions of flowers and leaves on the paisley motif, then work them with embroidery cotton (floss), using lazy-daisy stitch for the petals and leaves and small cross stitches for the flower centres (see pages 10-11). Turn under a small hem along the straight edge of each front shape and secure with blanket stitch.

4 Pin the fronts to the back with wrong sides facing and raw edges matching and stitch around the edges with blanket stitch in tapestry wool (yarn).

Nightdress case

♥

WHAT YOU NEED:

Scissors • Tape measure

Pre-washed and dyed

woollen blanket

Fusible bonding

Iron • Felt

Dressmaker's chalk pencil

Sewing thread and pins

Pre-gathered lace edging

Stranded embroidery

cotton (floss)

Embroidery needle

Tapestry wool (yarn)

Poppers

1 Cut a 32 x 38cm (12^1/$_2$ x 15in) rectangle of blanket for the nightdress case back. For the front, cut two pieces of blanket, each two-thirds the size of the nightdress case back (see page 16).

2 Trace two paisley motifs (see page 124) onto fusible bonding and iron the bonding onto felt. Cut out the shapes, peel away the backing and arrange the shapes on one of the front pieces. Iron the shapes in place, then secure with machine stitches. With a chalk pencil draw round the shape with a curl spiralling from the top, then pin and machine stitch the lace edging along this line.

3 Mark the flowers and leaves on the appliquéd shapes with the chalk pencil. Use embroidery cotton (floss) to work the petals and leaves in lazy-daisy stitch and each flower centre with a small cross stitch (see pages 10-11). Work a border of flowers and leaves along the lower long edge of the appliquéd front. Hem one long edge of each front shape and secure with blanket stitch in wool (yarn).

4 Pin the fronts to the back with wrong sides facing and raw edges matching and stitch around the edges with blanket stitch in tapestry wool (yarn). Attach the poppers to the front opening.

Christmas trimmings

*f*ill your home with festive cheer by making these wonderful Christmas decorations from old woollen blankets, hessian (jute), calico and felt, decorated with buttons, bells and braids. Simple sewing and embroidery techniques are all you need to create this colourful collection of Christmas cards, tree decorations, stockings, a hanging garland and a beautiful Christmas banner. All the projects use the same heart, star, holly, tree and stocking templates enlarged or reduced to different sizes.

Christmas stocking

WHAT YOU NEED:

Photocopies of small star and Christmas templates (see pages 120 and 126)
Scissors
Pre-washed woollen blanket or hessian (jute) base fabric
Contrasting fabric for the stocking tops (cuffs)
Sewing thread • Pins
Lace • Ricrac braid
Stranded embroidery cotton (floss)
Embroidery needle
Fusible bonding • Iron
Felt scraps • Buttons

1 Use the photocopied stocking as a pattern to cut two stockings of base fabric – one for the front and one for the back. Cut the top of the stocking again from contrasting fabric to make one cuff.

2 Topstitch the cuff to the top edge of the stocking front. Pin and then stitch on lace and braid along the bottom cuff edge to secure it to the stocking, then stitch lengths of braid across the stocking front to divide it into three sections. Work a row of cross stitches (see page 10) across the cuff with embroidery cotton (floss).

3 Cut out the photocopied templates and use them as patterns to trace your chosen motifs onto fusible bonding; iron the bonding onto felt scraps. Cut out the shapes, peel away the backing and arrange them on the stocking front. Iron the shapes to fuse them in place, then hand stitch around the edges with running stitches in embroidery cotton (floss). Stitch on buttons and work small straight-stitch stars with embroidery cotton (floss) for decoration, if required. (See pages 10-11 for details on working embroidery stitches.)

4 Pin the front and back stockings together with right sides facing. Machine stitch around the curved edges, leaving the top edge open. Clip the seam allowances where necessary for ease. Stitch a small hem along the top edge, then turn right sides out. Stitch a braid hanging loop to the top-back corner to hang the stocking.

Christmas banner

WHAT YOU NEED:

Scissors • Tape measure

Pre-washed woollen blanket

Hessian (jute)

Pinking shears (optional)

Felt scraps

Dressmaker's chalk pencil

Gold stranded embroidery

cotton (floss)

Embroidery needle • Calico

Needle and thread

Buttons

Fusible bonding • Iron

Bells • Stick

1 Cut a piece of blanket for backing the size you want your banner, and two 5 x 14cm (2 x 5½in) rectangles for hanging loops; trim the edges with pinking shears, if you have them, then cut shapes out of hessian (jute) slightly smaller than the blanket shapes.

2 Cut a felt patch and trim the edges with pinking shears, if you have them. Use a chalk pencil to write 'Merry Christmas' on the patch, then work backstitches (see page 10) with gold embroidery cotton (floss) over the chalk lines.

3 Cut a patch of calico slightly larger than the felt patch and lay this centrally over the hessian (jute). Pin the embroidered felt patch right side up over the calico patch. Work running stitches with embroidery cotton (floss) close to the edge of the felt patch, through all three layers. Stitch a button to each corner, then tease out the threads on the calico patch to fray the edges.

4 Trace the small star from page 120 and the holly and berry (page 126) as many times as you wish onto fusible bonding. Iron the bonding onto the felt scraps, cut out the shapes, peel away the backing and arrange the shapes on the large piece of hessian (jute). Iron them in place and secure with running stitches (see page 11) using embroidery cotton (floss). Stitch a button at the centre of each star.

5 Lay the hessian (jute) right side up over the blanket. Pin and stitch in place with two rows of running stitch in stranded cotton (floss). Finish the outer edges of the hessian (jute) by teasing out the threads to fray the edges, then stitch small bells at each corner. For the hanging loops, lay the hessian strips over the blanket strips, stitch in place and fray the edges. Fold them in half so the short edges meet, stitch to the top of the banner, then hang on a stick.

Christmas-tree decorations

WHAT YOU NEED:

Paper and pencil

Scissors • Felt

Stranded embroidery

cotton (floss)

Embroidery needle • Buttons

Polyester wadding (batting)

Metallic threads

1 Trace the large star, tree and heart shapes from pages 120 and 126 onto paper. Cut out the paper shapes and use them as patterns to cut two felt shapes for each decoration – one for the front and one for the back. On each front piece, stitch on buttons and embroider small straight-stitch stars with metallic thread (see page 11).

2 Pin the front and back shapes together, right sides out, then work blanket stitch (see page 10) around the edges with embroidery cotton (floss), leaving a gap for stuffing. Fill with wadding (batting), then complete the blanket stitching. Stitch a metallic thread hanging loop to the top of the padded decoration.

Christmas stocking garland

WHAT YOU NEED:

Paper and pencil
Scraps of pre-washed
woollen blanket, fabric
or hessian
Lace • Coloured braids
Sewing thread • Pins
Baubles • Flat braid

1 Trace the stocking from page 126 and use it to cut two fabric or blanket shapes for each stocking – one for the front and one for the back. Stitch rows of braids and lace to the stocking fronts.

2 Pin the front and back shapes together with right sides facing, then machine stitch around the curved edges, leaving the top edge open. Clip the seam allowances where necessary for ease. Stitch a small hem along the top edge, then turn the stocking right sides out. Stitch a braid hanging loop and bauble to the top-back edge.

3 Make several stockings in the same way. Cut the flat braid to the required length, tie a loop at each end, stitch the stockings along the braid, then hang the garland from the loops at each end.

Christmas cards

WHAT YOU NEED:

Card rectangles (A4 size
is ideal)
Hessian (jute) or calico
Photocopies or tracings of
star or Christmas templates
(see pages 120 and 126)
Fusible bonding • Iron
Felt scraps • Scissors
Gold stranded embroidery
cotton (floss)
Embroidery needle
Ribbon and braid scraps
(optional)
Buttons (optional)
Sewing thread

1 Fold each card in half so the short edges meet. Cut a piece of hessian (jute) or calico slightly smaller than the card.

2 Cut out the photocopied or traced holly and berry, tree or star template(s) and trace onto fusible bonding. Iron the bonding onto the wrong side of felt scraps, cut out the shapes, peel away the backing and arrange the fabric shapes on the hessian (jute) or calico. Iron the shapes to fuse them in place, then work running stitch (see page 11) around each shape using embroidery cotton (floss). Finally, stitch buttons, braid and/or ribbons in place.

3 Lay the appliquéd fabric right side up over the card and machine stitch 1cm (1/2in) from each edge of the fabric. Finish the outer edges by teasing out the threads to fray them. Write your message inside the card.

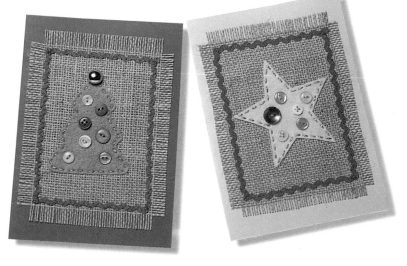

Royal chess set

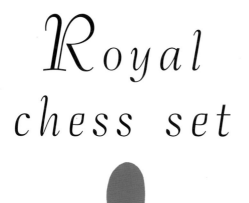

*I*f you like chess, you'll love this collection which centres on a chess board you can roll up and carry about with you. There's also a bag for the pieces and two cushions to sit on while you play. Decorated with crowns and fleur-de-lys in rich yellows and strong reds, the collection has a very regal feel. Yet as usual, many of the fabrics are recycled and the techniques are simple – the squares and motifs on the chessboard were created with potato prints and fabric paints.

WHAT YOU NEED:

Square cushion pad
Paper and pencil
Pre-washed and dyed
woollen blanket or velvet
Backing fabric
Photocopy of crown and
fleur-de-lys templates
(see page 125)
Fusible bonding • Iron
Contrasting fabric scraps
Scissors • Sewing thread
Pins • Ricrac braid
Twisted cord • Buttons

Tied cushion

1 On a piece of paper draw a square the size of your cushion pad. Draw a curved line to extend the corners by about 6.5cm (2$^{1}/_{2}$in), then add 1.5cm ($^{5}/_{8}$in) seam allowances all the way round. Use this as a pattern to cut a piece from blanket or velvet for the cushion front. For the cushion back cut two pieces of backing fabric, each two-thirds the size of the cushion front (see page 16).

2 On paper draw a small square to use as a pattern. Cut out the photocopied motifs and use them to trace the crown or fleur-de-lys and four small squares onto fusible bonding; iron the bonding onto contrasting fabric. Cut out the shapes, peel away the backing and arrange them centrally on the cushion front. Iron the shapes in place and secure with machine stitches, then stitch decorative braid around the edges of each shape. Add an extra row of braid across the crown, and decorate the points with buttons.

3 For the cushion back, stitch a narrow hem along one long edge of each back piece. Lay the appliquéd front right side up, then pin the back pieces right side down on top so that the raw outer edges match and the hemmed edges overlap at the centre.

4 Pin and tack (baste) the layers in place, then stitch around the outer straight and curved edges, taking a 1.5cm ($^{5}/_{8}$in) seam allowance. Clip the seam allowances at the corners for ease. Turn the cover right sides out, wrap twisted cord around each corner then insert the cushion pad.

Chess bag

WHAT YOU NEED:

Scissors • Tape measure
Check fabric
Fusible bonding • Iron
Fabric scrap
Sewing thread and pins
Decorative braid
Twisted cord

1 Cut a 25 x 58cm (9³/₄ x 22³/₄in) rectangle of check fabric. With wrong sides facing, fold the fabric in half so the short edges meet. The fold is the bottom of the bag. Cut two 5 x 23cm (2 x 9in) strips of check fabric for the drawstring channels.

2 Trace the crown motif from page 125 onto fusible bonding. Iron the bonding onto the wrong side of a fabric scrap, cut out the crown, peel away the backing and lay the crown above the fold on the check rectangle. Iron the shape in place, then unfold the bag and secure the crown with machine stitching. Stitch braid around the edges for decoration, if desired.

3 To make the drawstring channels, press a 1cm (¹/₂in) turning all the way round each channel strip. With right sides up, centre a channel strip over the rectangle, 4cm (1¹/₂in) from each short edge. Pin and tack (baste) the strips in place and stitch along the long edges, leaving the short edges open so that the twisted cord can be threaded through.

4 With right sides facing, bring the short edges of the bag fabric together. Pin and stitch the two side seams, taking a 1.5cm (⁵/₈in) seam allowance. Trim the seam allowances at the corners. Turn the bag right sides out, then stitch a 1.5cm (⁵/₈in) hem along the top edge. To finish the bag, cut two lengths of twisted cord, thread each one through both channels and knot the ends together. Fill the bag with your chess pieces.

Calico chess board

1 Cut two 52 x 62cm (20 1/2 x 24 1/2in) rectangles of calico and one of felt. On one calico rectangle use a ruler and chalk pencil to draw a 40cm (16in) square at the centre.

2 Trace and cut out the small crown on page 125 and cut out your photocopy of the other crown. Draw and cut out a large 5cm (2in) square and two smaller 1.5cm (5/8in) and 2cm (3/4in) squares. Cut each shape as a potato block (see page 12).

3 To print the chess-board chequers, take the large square potato block, and use a paintbrush to paint fabric paint onto the shape. Using the chalk lines as a guide, print a row of eight alternate squares for the chess-board chequers. Continue printing with the potato block until you have eight rows of eight squares altogether, then leave the paint to dry.

4 Use your other potato blocks to print a decorative row of crowns and medium-sized squares along both short edges of the calico rectangle then, using the smallest square, print a diamond shape at the centre of each coloured chequer. When all the paint is dry, use a brush to paint a contrasting dot at the corner of each decorative square and at the crown tips. Leave to dry then press the calico from the wrong side to fix the paints.

5 Stitch decorative braid around the outer edge of the chess board chequers, using the chalk lines as your guides. Lay the completed design right side up over the felt rectangle, then lay the remaining calico rectangle on top of the completed design. Pin and machine stitch around the edges, leaving a gap for turning. Trim the seam allowances at the corners for ease. Turn the chess board right sides out, machine stitch close to the edges, closing the gap as you do so, then stitch some more decorative braid close to the stitched edges as the final touch.

Patterns and templates

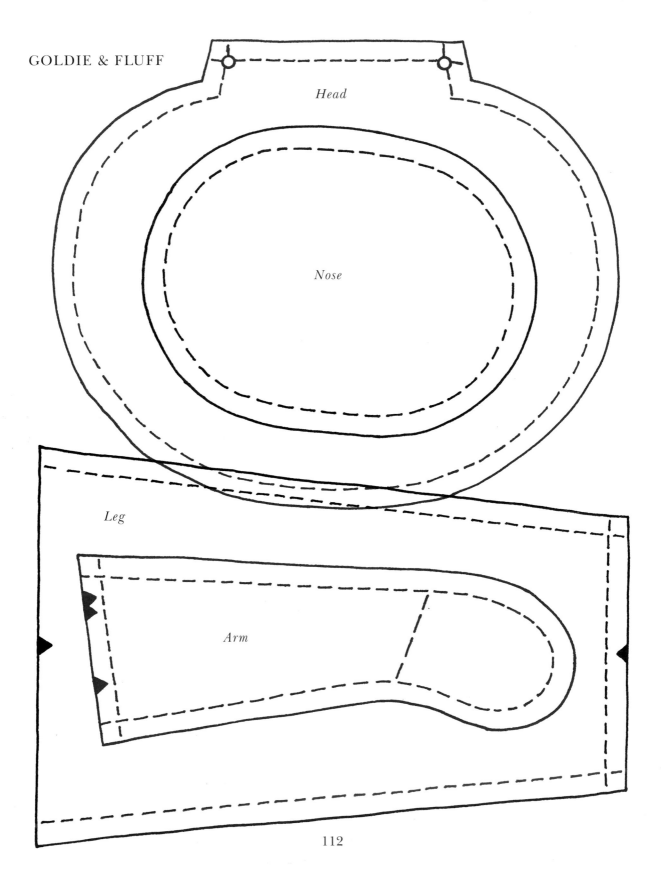

Head

Nose

Leg

Arm

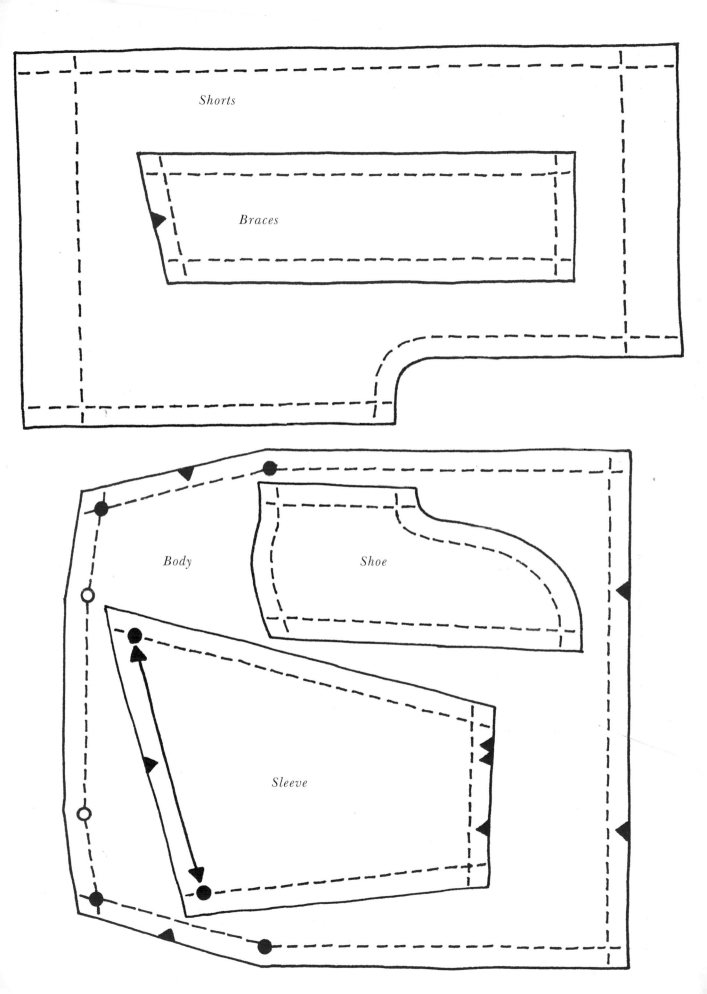

Shorts

Braces

Body

Shoe

Sleeve

FLOWERS & BEES

SUNFLOWER LEAF

SUNFLOWER
Place mat enlarge
148%; teapot stand and
flowerpot flowers 100%;
tea-cosy and carrier-bag
holder reduce to 76%

BUNNY: Drawstring bag enlarge
142%; Easter card 100%; badge
reduce to 69%

WASHING:
100%

Grass

LARGE CAT: *doorstop, enlarge 140%; calico cat 100%*

MEDIUM CAT: *juggling cat, cat picture and keepsake 100%*

SMALL CAT: *fridge magnet, wedding picture and cat picture 100%;*

PARTY HAT: card
100% and 147%

CAKE: card 100% and
enlarge base piece 143%

SMALL HORSESHOE:
card and wedding
picture 100%

LARGE HORSESHOE: keep-
sake and card 100%

GHOST: card enlarge
140%; bag and
wreath 100%

PUMPKIN: card, bag and wreath
100% and enlarge 138%

BAT: wreath enlarge 134%; bag
100% and reduce to 70%

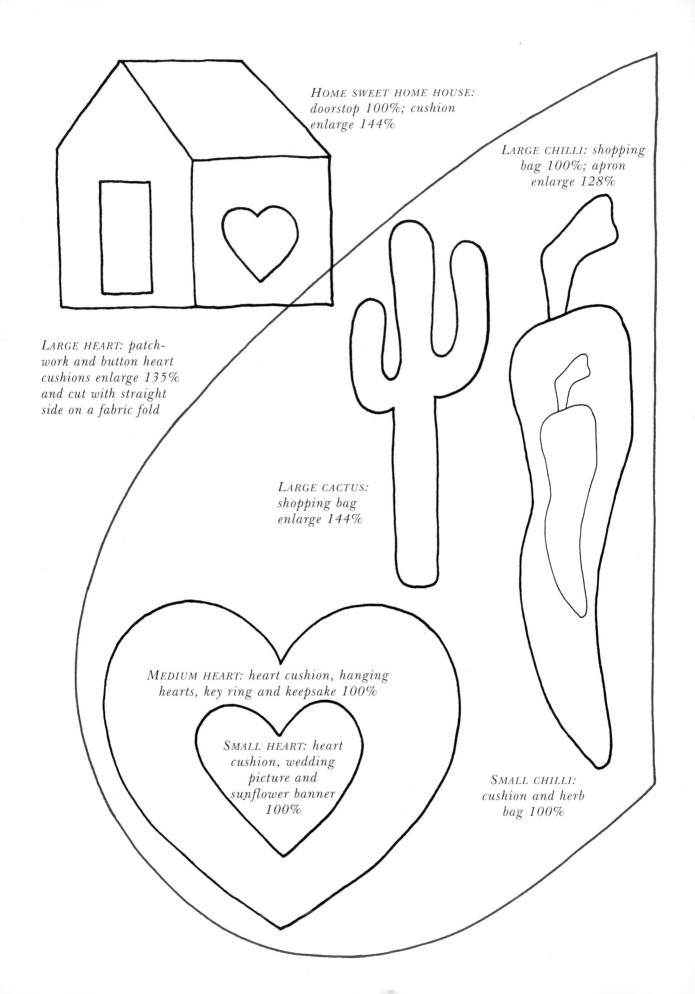

HOME SWEET HOME HOUSE:
doorstop 100%; cushion
enlarge 144%

LARGE CHILLI: shopping
bag 100%; apron
enlarge 128%

LARGE HEART: patch-
work and button heart
cushions enlarge 135%
and cut with straight
side on a fabric fold

LARGE CACTUS:
shopping bag
enlarge 144%

MEDIUM HEART: heart cushion, hanging
hearts, key ring and keepsake 100%

SMALL HEART: heart
cushion, wedding
picture and
sunflower banner
100%

SMALL CHILLI:
cushion and herb
bag 100%

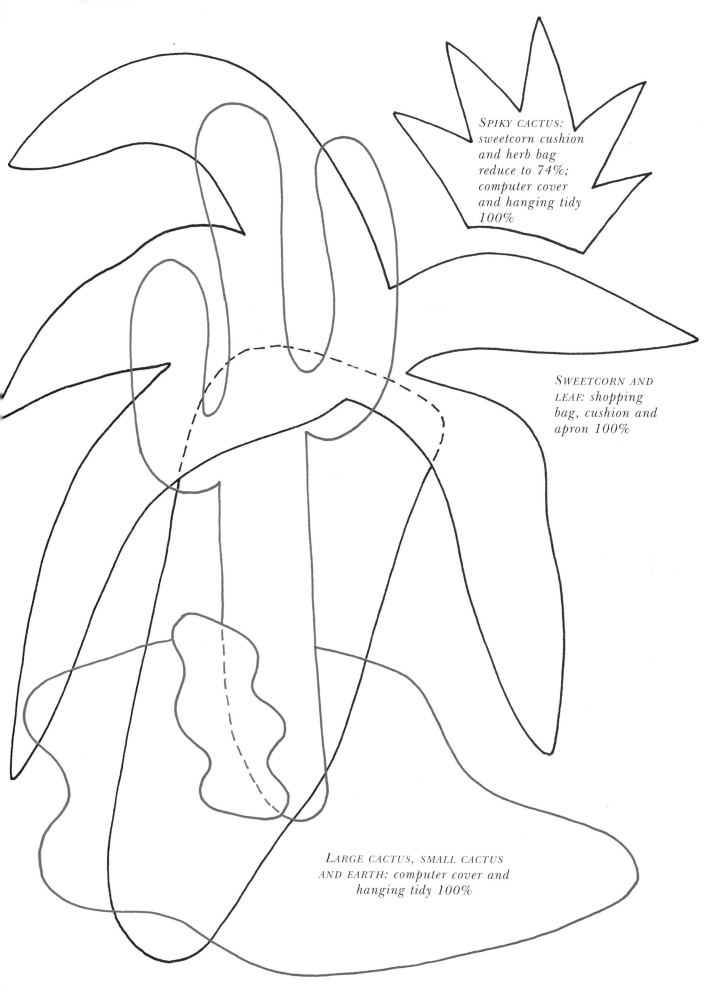

SPIKY CACTUS:
sweetcorn cushion
and herb bag
reduce to 74%;
computer cover
and hanging tidy
100%

SWEETCORN AND
LEAF: shopping
bag, cushion and
apron 100%

LARGE CACTUS, SMALL CACTUS
AND EARTH: computer cover and
hanging tidy 100%

LARGE MOON:
patchwork cot
cover 100%

LARGE STAR: cot cover, mobile,
hanging stars, Christmas-tree
decorations and cards,
windbreak, beach bag and
beach towel reduce to 71%;
star garland, windbreak, beach
bag, starlight picture and bedspread 100%; star and starfish
cushions increase until centre
line is 43cm (17in)

SMALL STAR: Christmas
banner and starlight picture
100%; mobile appliqué, cot
cover, beach towel, beach
bag and Christmas stocking
enlarge 144%

SMALL MOON: patchwork
cot cover 100%; mobile
reduce to 75%

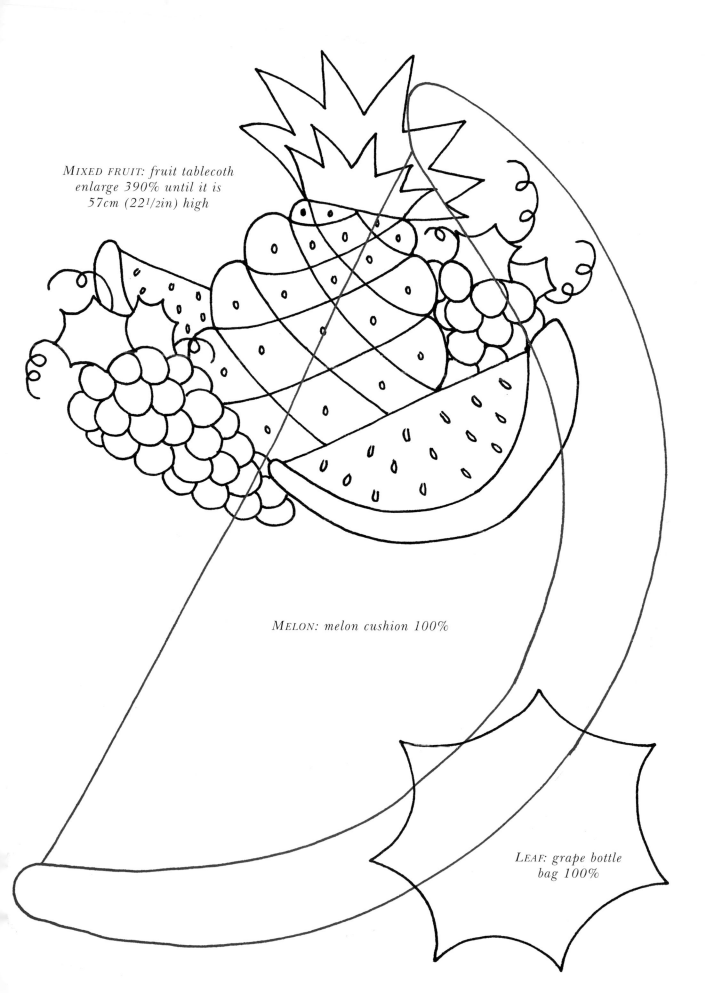

MIXED FRUIT: *fruit tablecoth enlarge 390% until it is 57cm (22^1/$_2$in) high*

MELON: *melon cushion 100%*

LEAF: *grape bottle bag 100%*

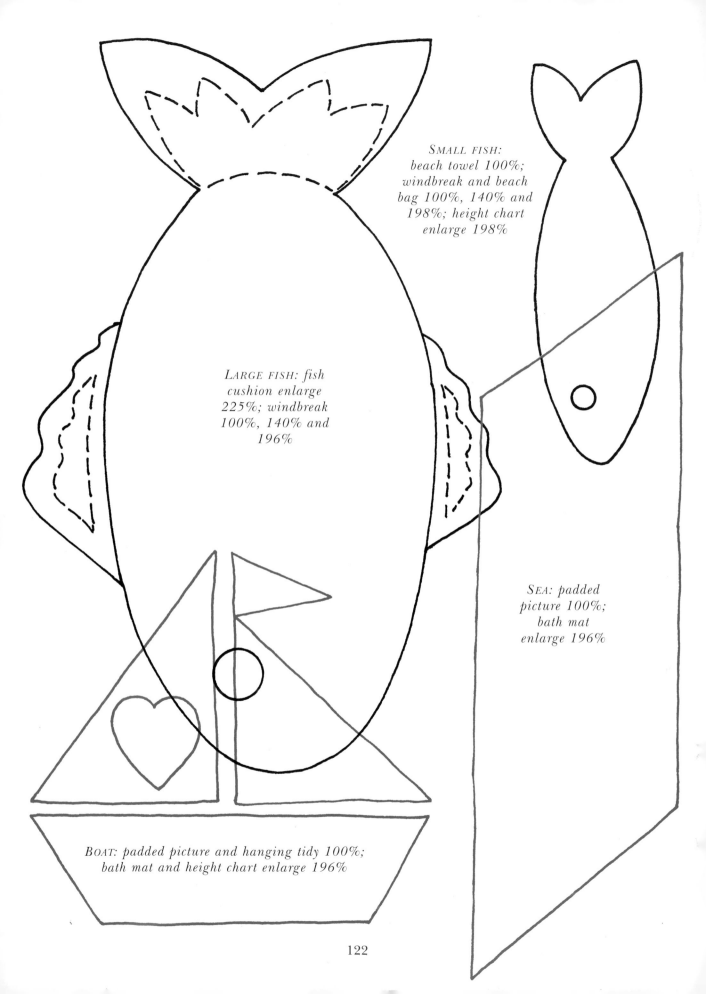

SMALL FISH:
beach towel 100%;
windbreak and beach
bag 100%, 140% and
198%; height chart
enlarge 198%

LARGE FISH: *fish*
cushion enlarge
225%; windbreak
100%, 140% and
196%

SEA: *padded*
picture 100%;
bath mat
enlarge 196%

BOAT: *padded picture and hanging tidy 100%;*
bath mat and height chart enlarge 196%

CLOUD: *padded picture reduce to 81%; hanging tidies, computer cover and sweetcorn cushion 100%; bath mat and height chart enlarge 170%*

SAD OLD BEAR: *bear picture 100%; bear pyjama case enlarge 140%*

SUN: *height chart enlarge 136%; hanging tidies and computer cover 100%*

SMALL SUN: *herb bag and sweetcorn cushion 100%*

AUTUMN RABBIT CUSHIONS:
enlarge to fit your cushion

PAISLEY: cushion,
water-bottle cover
and nightdress case
100%

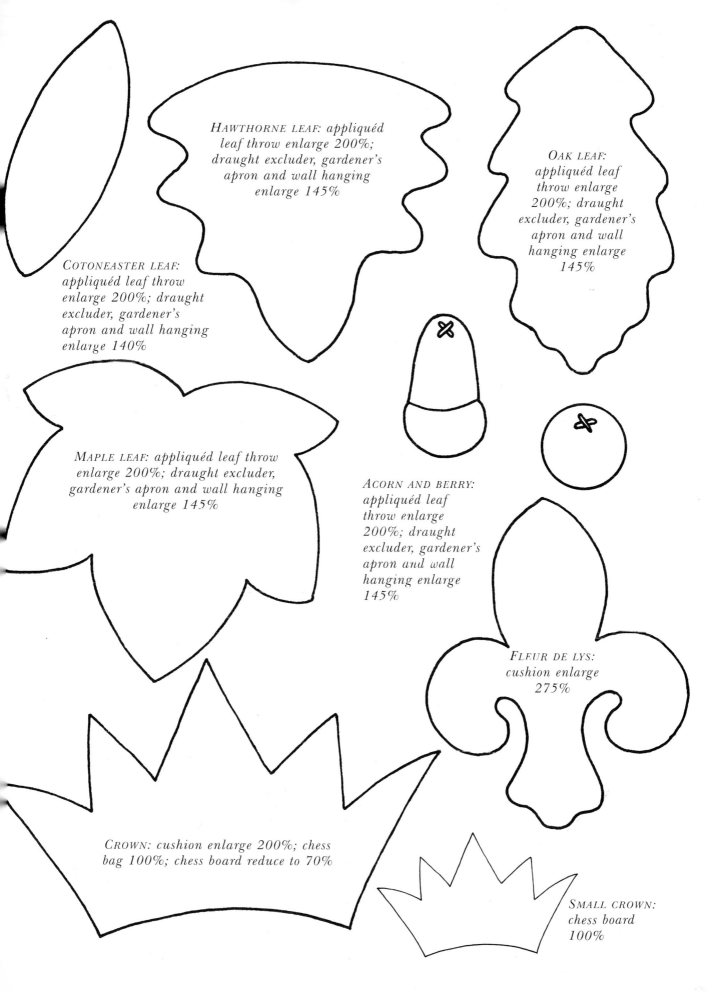

HAWTHORNE LEAF: appliquéd leaf throw enlarge 200%; draught excluder, gardener's apron and wall hanging enlarge 145%

OAK LEAF: appliquéd leaf throw enlarge 200%; draught excluder, gardener's apron and wall hanging enlarge 145%

COTONEASTER LEAF: appliquéd leaf throw enlarge 200%; draught excluder, gardener's apron and wall hanging enlarge 140%

MAPLE LEAF: appliquéd leaf throw enlarge 200%; draught excluder, gardener's apron and wall hanging enlarge 145%

ACORN AND BERRY: appliquéd leaf throw enlarge 200%; draught excluder, gardener's apron and wall hanging enlarge 145%

FLEUR DE LYS: cushion enlarge 275%

CROWN: cushion enlarge 200%; chess bag 100%; chess board reduce to 70%

SMALL CROWN: chess board 100%

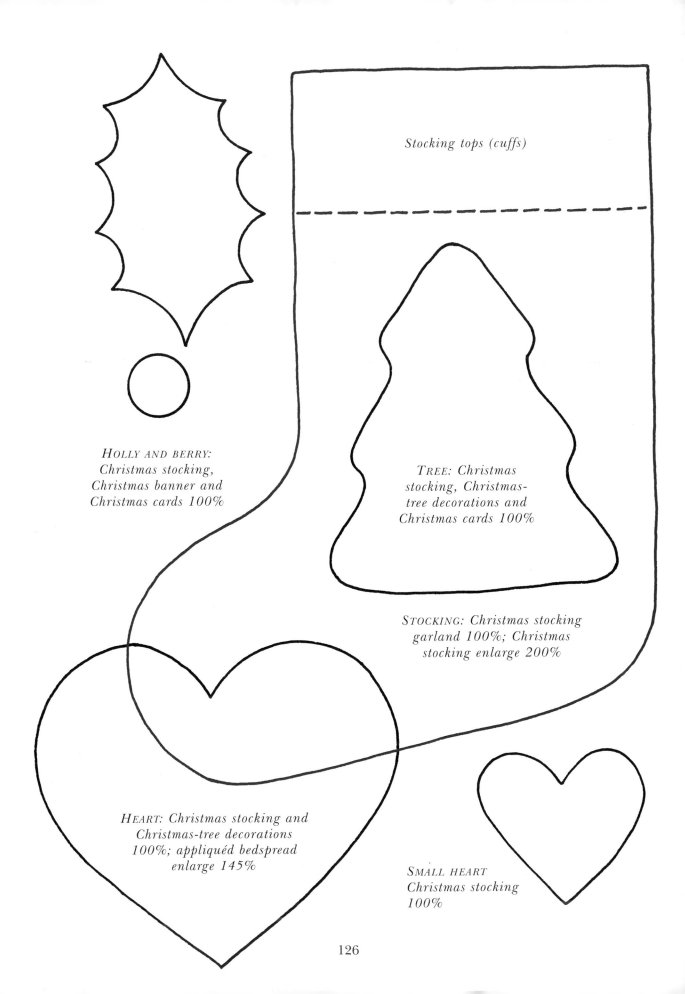

Stocking tops (cuffs)

HOLLY AND BERRY: *Christmas stocking, Christmas banner and Christmas cards 100%*

TREE: *Christmas stocking, Christmas-tree decorations and Christmas cards 100%*

STOCKING: *Christmas stocking garland 100%; Christmas stocking enlarge 200%*

HEART: *Christmas stocking and Christmas-tree decorations 100%; appliquéd bedspread enlarge 145%*

SMALL HEART *Christmas stocking 100%*

Stockists

If you want any further information about the products used in this book, catalogues, price lists or local stockists from any of the suppliers listed, contact them direct by post or phone. Please remember to include a stamped-addressed envelope with postal enquiries. If you contact them by phone, they will be able to tell you if there is any charge for the catalogue or price list.

THREADS AND YARN

All projects in this book use DMC stranded embroidery cottons (floss), metallic threads and tapestry wool (yarn). The shade numbers of the threads used have not been given because you can use up scraps or choose colours to match your fabrics.

DMC Creative World, Pullman Road, Wigston, Leicester LE18 2DY. Tel: 0116 281 1040.
Write or phone for the name and address of your nearest DMC stockists.

DMC products are also available world-wide from:
USA   The DMC Corporation, Port Kearny, Building 10, South Kearny, NJ 07032.
Tel: 001 201 589 0606 / 001 201 589 8931.
Australia   DMC, 51-66 Carrington Road, Marrickville, New South Wales 2204.
Tel: 00 612 559 3088 / 00 612 559 5338.

South Africa   S A T C, 43 Somerset Road, PO Box 3868, Capetown 8000.
Tel: 00 272 141 98040.
Hong Kong   DMC Hong Kong, Rem. 1311, Austin Tower, 22 Austin Avenue, Tsimshatsui, Kowloon. Tel: 00 852 367 1896.

FUSIBLE BONDING AND WASHABLE FELT

For appliqué all projects use Bondaweb fusible bonding. Bondaweb is a brand name used in the UK. Some of the projects use Funtex washable felt. Funtex is another brand name used in the UK. These products are both made by **Vilene.** Vilene products are available in major department stores and all good haberdashery shops.

DYES, PAINTS AND MARKER PENS

Dylon fabric dyes, Colour Fun marker pens and paints were used on projects throughout the book. They are available from major department stores and all good haberdashery shops.

DYLON International Ltd., Worsley Bridge Road, Lower Sydenham, London SE26 5HD.
Tel: 0181 663 4801.
Write or phone for the name and address of your nearest Dylon stockists.

ACKNOWLEDGMENTS

This book was completed in double-quick time, and I would like to give a big thank you to everyone who helped and contributed to this book, especially: Cheryl Brown, Kay Ball, Brenda Morrison and Jane Trollope at David & Charles for their help, guidance and support with the production of this book. Cara Ackerman, Susan Haigh and Sam Ruston for supplying products and materials when I always needed them URGENTLY! Di Lewis for the beautiful photography. It always brightened up my day to look at the transparencies when they dropped through the letter box. Thank you also to Steve Beer for the photography on the back cover flap. Doreen Montgomery for her help, support and encouraging letters, which I always love to receive. A big thank you to Fluff and Goldie and the rest of my family for being so patient and understanding, and a special thank you to Timmy, my long-suffering husband. Finally my cats, Pip and Felix need to be remembered for keeping me company, helping with the writing by walking all over my keyboard and playing with the mouse, playing with my threads and sleeping in the fabric box.

Index